Get My

S.H.I.T.

Together

The Straight Talk Playbook for
Creating a Life Worth Living

Lerrod E. Smalls

Published by Lion Spirit Publishing

Lion Spirit Publishing

1704 Flatbush Ave.

Brooklyn, NY 11210

www.GetMyShitTogether.com

GMSTresults@Gmail.com

ISBN: 978-1-7333412-1-9

Second Edition: September 2024

Get My S.H.I.T. Together

The Straight Talk Playbook for Creating a Life Worth Living

"A man won't make a change until the pain of things staying the same becomes greater than the pain of making the change."

- Tony Robbins remixed by Lerrod

Table of Contents

BIG THANKS,

To give justice and thank everyone properly that has played a crucial part in my life and this book, would take another book just as thick as this one. It's hard to stop smiling as I think about the insane stories of reckless times and near-fatal calamities that I've survived with many of these nameless people, who are probably just as surprised as I am that we made it through. This is not a memoir or some tell-all exposing the people and crazy things we have been through. These are the boiled-down salt lessons from my experiences. I would like to name a few people specifically who have made very specific contributions to this book because it is just as much theirs as well.

My wife, Qahira Smalls, is the most important human being to me in this world. We are so imperfectly perfect for each other. Many of the reasons why I was committed enough to see this project through was because you boldly endured the worst of my S.H.I.T. Thank you for trusting me, forgiving me, following me, supporting me, and above all loving me. My greatest hope for each of my kids is that they will find their very own Q, because with that alone, I'll know they will be alright.

Big thanks to the Black Warrior King tribesman, who have been with me since my rebirth, and continue to hold me accountable to who I say I am. Salute to all of the KINGS near and far who have allowed me to serve them, because I have drawn strength and experience from your sharing and vulnerability. Endless thanks to my coaches and community, who have all contributed to my growth and development. I am also very grateful to everyone who has cheered me on through social media, giving me feedback and fuel to keep sharing my ideas. Special thanks to Sherod Khaalis, Rob Huxley, and Cassandra Cousineau who have both invested uncounted hours of their lives listening to me rant and helping me get clear through scores of revisions of this project. And finally, my aunt Lynelle, who unofficially took on the role of being my mom since the very day I lost my first mother. I could not repay you for your generosity and commitment, but I'll honor you by paying it forward.

Salute to YOU, for considering this book worthy of your time; I am grateful.

Lerrod E. Smalls

"It's two things he gets every day when he wakes up.

A chance and a choice. The choices that he makes
after he gets his chance...that's on him;

he'll have to live with that."

- J. Prince

INTRODUCTION

Sorry, Not Sorry

This book ain't for everybody. As a matter of fact, it's not for most people. The title alone is designed to ward off any 'Mr. Goody Two-Shoes' that would even think about picking it up! My guess is since you've made it this far, you're probably thinking to yourself, "Whatever advice he has to give can't possibly make things worse!" And that's a FACT. Nobody picks up a book titled Get My S.H.I.T. Together if they think they already have their S.H.I.T. together. So, I'm going to assume that you don't have your S.H.I.T. together and much rather wish that you did. This book is for men who know they have fucked up and believe there must be another way. These men understand the longer they wait to resolve their S.H.I.T., the harder it will be to do so.

If my only goal were to sell lots of books, then this would not be the one I'm publishing. To reach the biggest buying audience, I could have created a politically correct memoir of rags to riches that's full of bible quotes and scrabble words. DEFINITELY NOT THIS BOOK. My intention is to provide a bullshit-free playbook to help 'guys like us' find our way back into a life worth living. To accomplish this, I will show you my scars and tell you how I got cut so that you can avoid my mistakes. I am not a motivational guru looking to mystify you with verbal judo. This is likely the reason I struggled for three years writing and rewriting, thinking it could never be good enough.

The concepts laid out in this project will work for every gender, race, creed, and even aliens. But this book is specifically designed to speak to men. I am writing this book exactly as I would have been prepared to receive the information. Imagine a future version of yourself sent back to tell you how to navigate past all the mistakes you made. For those with eyes to see and ears to hear, this book could be the difference between life and death - literally. However, I will spend zero time or words trying to persuade you to believe this information. But here's a fun fact for you to digest:

Bees don't waste time explaining to Flies why honey is better than shit!

You are about to step into a war, so expect to fight for every square inch of the life that life you say you want. No stimulus, freebies, or handouts are available for a life worth living. Everything will cost you a sacrifice and require a commitment. The good news is you don't have to go at this alone. I will be with you. You will also have the option to join the ranks with other kings in the G.M.S.T. (Get My Shit Together) community. This is where men are empowered and encouraged to develop into the true leaders that we were all born to be. It's time for honesty, strict action, and real results.

Here is a hard truth: too many men are suffering lives of quiet desperation. These men feel lost and alone but are too suffocated by the perception of their situation to make a change. So, let's take "What is a Man's Ego" for five hundred Alex (in my Jeopardy voice.) I was that lost soul, feeling confused and suffocated by the life I created. My journey has taken me through bankruptcy, a marriage on the brink of divorce, and suicidal desperation. Living in a perpetual hurricane of what-the-fuck, until the day I decided to take accountability for my own life and execute some new thinking. No motivational seminar bullshit, just proven strategies to live as a real man. Ready for anything and everything. A warrior. These came from lessons not handed down to me from generations of knowledge by my ancestors but hard-earned through the painful evolutions of experience. I sacrificed everything to have a whole new life. It was worth it.

Starting my life over at 40, I became an IBJJF world champion in Ju Jitsu, a personal development coach, a real estate developer, and, as of now, a 2x author. This enabled me to purchase a beautiful home and retire my wife 30 years ahead of schedule. Become a healthy father, husband, and entrepreneur all at the same time. I've created a lifestyle of abundance and purpose. Repeatable action steps have led me down an incredible path of recovery into dominance while maintaining a balanced life of happiness along the way! There is no magic here, only principles and processes. However, it began with the realization that I was the only person responsible for Getting My S.H.I.T Together! The acronym S.H.I.T (Story, Health, Income & Time) is the functional keys referred to as controls that we will use to unlock the potential in our lives. I will share why it is required to thoroughly understand each one and provide the steps I have used to dominate in each of these areas. This is not a game of perfection, where you must become like Yoda of the S.H.I.T. force. Also, no one is getting fixed here because YOU ARE NOT BROKEN. This is not a one-size-fits-all cure for life's bullshit that solves your problems forever. GMST (get my S.H.I.T. Together) is a lifestyle!

If what I have shared so far resonates, and my word choices haven't totally pissed you off, then we have a solid chance of working together. Now here is an absolute truth, the moment that you sink your teeth into these concepts that I've painstakingly put together, something will interrupt you. The ding from your phone, the dog pissed in the house, a news update for the latest world catastrophe; whatever can distract you will try. SO, protect this opportunity by secluding and boxing yourself in for the next five chapters. Do it like your life is on the line... Because, like I said before, it is.

At the end of every chapter, I will take you to a BATTLEGROUND. This is an opportunity to challenge the subject from a different perspective, followed by Power Action Steps. Take it seriously. These will be "versus battles" between forces, ideas, and concepts that men like us must contend with. These are the things that will stop you from becoming who you must be to win. However, you will never win them all, and you will always have to battle with something to keep your S.H.I.T. together... BUT IT'S ALL ABOUT THE WAR! The long game. Consistently winning more battles than you lose, tipping the scales toward a life worth living, one which you can look back on and be proud of someday.

Next Up, I will let you into my personal S.H.I.T. show.

HIS-STORY

From Desperation to Dominance

It starts with me growing up at the crossroads of Brownsville and East Flatbush Brooklyn we called the 90s. Real ghetto. Our crime-infested **A**lleys, **B**uildings, and **C**orners were the first ABCs we had to learn. But for the most part, I loved growing up in Rutland Plaza. I can promise you this: my neighborhood provided an unlimited source of opportunities for life-altering danger and trouble. I found and experienced plenty of them. However, my parents were not deadbeats and made sure my sister and I could survive, have great memories, get into college, and position ourselves to be something. My father couldn't take the "IT" anymore and left my mother for another woman before I made the 1st grade. I shared a bedroom with my younger sister until I was 10. Back then, you could describe me as completely nerded out on comic books, small pets, and anything involving computers. Middle school was my introduction to cutting school, girls, weed, drinking, and modifying attendance cards successfully. High school marked the diagnosis of breast cancer for my mother, and in proper rebellious teenager form, I filled her plate with stress and terrible school performance. She shipped me off to finish high school with my father in Corona, Queens, which in retrospect, was a genius move. I had no choice but to get my S.H.I.T. together under the Rodney Smalls regime. Despite the consecutive series of summer school and night school during every remaining semester, I successfully graduated from Brooklyn Technical high school and went off to college.

Susquehanna University was in the middle of "no-black-people Pennsylvania", where I received a huge dose of culture shock but ultimately got an amazing education. I also wrestled varsity for two years, learned to river fish like a local, and sold copious amounts of weed to my schoolmates. My mom didn't get to witness the fruits of her labor. At 46 years old, she died in Sloan Kettering hospital one morning during the second semester of my sophomore year. That hurt. She was the most devout Christian I ever knew or could imagine. How could God let her die so young? She dedicated countless hours on her knees praying and a significant amount of her income to the church, but neither of those things saved my mom. I secretly resolved that if God wouldn't save an angel like her, he damn sure wouldn't be there for a heathen like me, so my faith was buried right along with Juanelle Smalls. Decades later, Bishop TD Jakes did an interview with Steve Harvey, where he told him something that impacted me very deeply and gave me a sense of peace. He said:

"If you deposit enough **INTO** your kids, you do not have to leave anything **TO THEM.** Because what you deposited **IN THEM** will allow them to get those things for themselves."

FACTS!

Early on, she heavily invested in teaching my sister and I the correct values. She fortified these values so that we could make our own way when she was gone. One day, in another book, I will go into much more depth on the pain of losing my mom and how it shaped my decisions for years, but for now I'm honoring her with my commitment to sharing my truth.

Six months on my grandmother's couch after graduating from college, I struck gold with a computer support job with a Fortune 100 bank on Wall Street. Followed by a few short years, which included the Y2K scare and the 9/11 tragedy, I was making an eighty thousand dollars salary and purchased my first house. All of this before my 25th birthday. I had a motorcycle, a beautiful girlfriend, and was built like an athlete. I was doing my thing. But then came the crash. I suffered whiplash like a motherfucker when I lost that job to some corporate merger layoff bullshit. I would have traded that experience for an actual car accident because my job was directly connected to my self-worth. It was me. I had assigned myself the value of that job. Working on Wall Street. was a big deal to me, and when I brandished my business card, even though my name was the smallest text printed on it, I was so proud of the association. But now, I had nothing. I lost my identity. Facing my monthly payments for college loans, mortgage, and alcohol with no income, was scary as hell. But I had a burning desire in my stomach that set me on fire.

I found something to hate! I hated not being in control of my income, and I would not allow circumstance to do that to me again. So, I launched my own business. Through God's perfect alignment of timing and positioning, I had recently reconnected with my high school friend Geno, and we were already working on something big. Geno had recently returned to Brooklyn from an educational stay with the New York State Dept of Corrections. And with all his in-depth incarceration experience, we decided to launch an online company, making it easy to send care packages to prisons. And so, we did. This would be the hardest thing we had ever done in our lives to this point.

So, what does a young man do when his back is up against the wall, and he is about to take on the biggest challenge of his life? You're right, He gets married. What a psycho Mrs. Smalls must have been to accept my proposal and get permanently hitched to a guy that just lost his job and promised to spend very little time with her as he built a new business that would soon become a second wife. Damn, she was a rock star.

I worked as a consultant fixing computers, installing security cameras, and picking up odd jobs to finance the website. Every penny I had saved or earned went pouring into this company, UpNorth Services. After a few short years (three exactly), we finally got to a position where we had some sales, and things were looking up. My newly minted wife was thoroughly disgusted with having a 24-hour online supermarket running out of the house, so I moved the business out of my basement into our first storefront. We only required a warehouse, but the location had a storefront, and since there was no post office within a 10-minute walk of the place, we started an entirely brand-new shipping business.

This was the time when my life was probably moving the fastest. I had never experienced this much money, business, respect, and honor from people around me. People thought of me as a businessman. I was an entrepreneur. I was the American dream. A young black kid from the ghetto goes to college, loses his dream job, but then recovers and becomes an entrepreneur success. DAMN! I impressed myself. Even telling this story right now, I feel like poking my chest out. But that story was short-lived because in 2008 - 2009, the economy took a massive shift. And because I was so thickheaded and I did not seek out good counsel from anyone besides myself, the whole ship went down. The boat started to sink, and I could not save it. So, I took every dime that I had and I leveraged it against my property. I did every little side project that I could think of, to come up with extra cash to funnel into my dying business.

I had not actually sought out real mentors and counsel to help me because I was hiding the fact that I didn't know what to do. I could not bear the idea of admitting that I was lost, alone, and about to fail at the one thing that gave my life significance. So, I just kept pouring more water into a leaking boat. And before I knew it, I was drowning.

I remember very clearly one morning, getting a phone call from my daughter's daycare center when they said, "Your daughter cannot be accepted to the school until you bring payment." With tears in my eyes and a lump in my throat, I took the gold chain off my neck, and I drove around at five o'clock in the morning, looking for a 24-hour pawn shop. Replying to my desperate outcry, I got a phone call from a friend who practically saved my life. Lesley Hope was an angel that morning when she offered to send me the money I needed to get my little girl past that Viking at the front desk. Praise God, even though it only stopped the bleeding for another week or so, saving face with my wife was the most important thing I could imagine at the time.

At this point, I decided it would be a great idea to start another business. I figured the recession must be killing my industry and I complained ad nauseam about the white man, taxes, employees, my partner, and the economy. I thought if only those things had changed, I could still be doing well. I began to resent my wife and kids because they seemed like burdens that I could no longer afford to carry. With that mentality and being distracted by everything that wasn't my business, I ultimately found myself in foreclosure, followed by bankruptcy. This was the darkest, most humbling point in my life. Going through the bankruptcy process was so hard for my ego that I wanted to just die and get it over with. I seriously considered it a few times. The thoughts of just letting myself go, driving off the Brooklyn Bridge, and hitting restart on life. My noose of consequences became so tight I couldn't breathe.

We moved out of my brownstone and in with my mother-in-law. We crammed our three kids into the guest room next to us, and we stayed in the bedroom she grew up in as a child. Heartbreaking. My wife and I argued all the time, and I found regular reasons to sleep in my car rather than come inside. It also became quite normal to dig through the console and under the seat of my BMW for loose change to put gas in the tank. My American dream had turned into a nightmare.

However, I am grateful for all the tragedy because it set off a revelation fire of biblical proportion. I realized there was no other choice than to get my S.H.I.T. together! I started consuming motivational podcasts, books, online courses, and all kinds of inspirational mojo CDs. I ran up the balances on my credit cards, going to networking events, seminars, conferences, and self-help media.

I had a natural talent for public speaking, which I perfected in network marketing, where I regurgitated everything I was learning into my sales meetings. (Here is a shameless plug: check out my book "Present Like a Pro for Networkers" on Amazon.) I was a damn good network marketer, by the way. Despite that fact, I was still tearing my S.H.I.T. down using every possible distraction, from seducing women in the meetings to drinking myself into a wildman at the club. I was completely sabotaging my marriage. Eating fast food all day with no time for exercise helped wrap a tire of fat around my midsection. I was fronting for people and trying to keep up the appearance that I had my S.H.I.T. together when I was just a bunch of broken pieces held together by GOD's grace.

I remember very clearly having both a fully loaded Hybrid Cadillac Escalade and a BMW 750 Li at the same time, but alternating which car note got paid from month to month. Alongside the truth that I would rack up parking tickets, not pay them, get towed, borrow money from my angel Nadina, aunt Lynnie, my father, or whoever else, go get the car back, and repeat this over and over again.

This continued to the point I couldn't make my payments, and I slipped into a cold war with Brooklyn's finest repo companies. From day to day, I used different parking garages, preferably underground and concrete, so the scanners and the satellites could not find my car. And I would leave it there all night until the repo companies would be off the streets. Then I would go get it and take it home and put it behind my wife's other car in her mother's driveway, praying that nobody was bold enough to find it and pull it out. That's how fucked up I was. That's how much I had to get my S.H.I.T. together. Beyond all of those things and figuring out ways to hustle and beat the system, I was seeking out support. I was looking, and then I found something.

In the still of the night, I watched some dramatic online video ad from a high-energy, bold, and charismatic white guy (literally named Mr. White) offering training and programs for men to resurrect their lives. This sounded amazing, but I knew it wasn't for me because I didn't see anybody in his videos that looked like me. So, I just watched and trolled him for about a year. I would share clips of videos with friends trying to get some confirmation or moral support that WE should do this together, but there were no takers. I kept up with the testimonials of men sharing stories of total transformation in their lives. I watched the confession videos of life dramas similar to mine, but I was stuck thinking that they just didn't look like me (ex-rich White men from God knows where USA). I assumed that their program wouldn't work for me (A black man from the hood) until one day, I had enough. Somewhere around one o'clock in the morning, I just made a decision. I'm going to hit the button, and I'm going to call and get into this fucking program. So, I filled out the online application and got a phone call from this guy with a Persian accent, speaking with certainty and confidence. He asked me short, powerful questions.

Sam was generous and listened quietly, giving me an opportunity to tell him my life story. Believe me, I poured out my fucking guts. I told him I felt alone and on the verge of dying, the fact that I cheated on my wife. I told him all about the bankruptcy and losing my company. I told him all about the shame of living with my mother-in-law and the fact my daughter and two sons shared a room. I explained how my wife used the same closet as when she was growing up. He listened quietly, then said bluntly, "You can't afford this program, and you're not ready for this step now." Then he gave me the number for the program; it was a nonrefundable ten thousand dollars. There was a brief pause where I was recovering from being struck right in the gut with disappointment. He followed up with, "Just download the

podcasts, listen to all the shows, and follow the message."
Then, that was it. he was gone.

The whole recount would not be important if not for this
next part. A few days later, I noticed Sam began following me
on Facebook. I took that as a sign of care and accountability,
which was just what I wanted. I decided to make some
serious fucking changes. I channeled my energy into long-
distance running while listening to those podcasts every day.
Garret White became my headphone mentor.

I worked my ass off learning how to live like a new man.
A warrior man who didn't accept bullshit from himself or
others. This forced me to stop lying long enough to see how I
was sabotaging myself with bad habits and weak choices.

I started with my beliefs around religion and compared it
to what was told to me as a child. I faced the truth about my
relationship with my kids, how I felt about my wife, our
communication, and my connection with her. I began to
accept the truth from the mirror about my fitness, finally
admitting I was fat and ashamed of my body. I started to tell
the truth about my finances and the fact that I was spending
money on expensive things and pretending to still have
money so that people would respect me.

All these truths made me realize that there was no way
out and no one was coming to save me! It was about time for

me to participate in my own rescue. So that's exactly what I did.

I became obsessed with making meaningful changes in my life, starting with one commitment. To stop lying and tell the truth. Which turned out to be much harder than I thought it would be. I started sharing with people close to me the truth of what was going on in my life, totally unashamed, like I didn't care. But just doing that improved my situation. A big fact to note is that the changes didn't happen overnight. Just like no one gets fat from eating one cheeseburger, you don't become healthy by eating one salad. I began building my new life around specific commitments and relentless consistency.

Next, I connected to the divine spirit inside myself. God is real. Many of my beliefs around religion had changed; however, my faith in God was totally renewed. I discovered that we were more than worthy of being happy; it is our right to be. I recovered my purpose for living like a favorite jacket in the lost and found. My reasons for achieving became bigger than my excuses for failing, and my to-do list became longer than my wish list. I started feeling joy again.

Although feeling good was great, it was not enough because I was still broke, fat, and lonely. I wanted my results to change. A new self-respect was required, and I was going to earn it. What I learned on my journey was a simple paint-by-numbers system of daily routines, which dramatically improved all of the important areas in my life. Taking small steps every day was better and led to better decisions. There was an actual duplicatable process I followed to have a powerful day every single day repeatedly and predictably. My guilt about what was before disappeared, and the worry about what was going to happen started to shrink. I could clearly see that taking small steps every single day moved me closer to the man that I wanted to become.

I rebuilt myself into a grateful, resourceful, excuseless, no-nonsense motherfucker. By recognizing my new power, I had confidence that I could achieve anything. And because I used simple but powerful routines, they have become habits I do instinctively daily. Anything that you do without thinking takes very little effort, and my progress was getting easier with time. From desperation to dominance, Growth and results began showing up in my life frequently and consistently.

Now, I live in a beautiful home, drive a beautiful truck, and take beautiful vacations with my beautiful family. Life is not perfect, but it is damn sure beautiful. My loving and connected relationship with my children matters more to me than anything in this world. This process of transformation is the best thing in the world since pockets in pants, and I have to share it! Every Brother, Husband, and Father should master the art of Get My S.H.I.T. Together. I can only imagine the tremendous impact of Dads all around the world teaching these tactics to their sons. It is my intention to pour into others what I know works, and to leave this world better than I found it.

So, if you can see yourself in that story in some way, and you're ready to get your S.H.I.T. together, then keep listening. If not, then you must be "good," and in that case, simply hit fast forward. I send you back in whatever direction you are going with blessings and good energy. This conversation is for a man on a comeback who is willing to believe that every setback is just a setup for a step up!

Enough chit-chat: it's go time!

CHAPTER ZERO
- THE GROUNDWORK

What is this S.H.I.T.?

There is no other word in the English language that has more application and diversity than the word shit. You can say Who, What, Where, When, and How - Is that Shit. There could be an entire book of definitions and use for the word as a verb, a noun, a pronoun, or an adjective because everything in this world can be considered shit. It just depends on the way you say it. There have been a few dope books that have crossed my path implying this word in the title, such as Get SH*T Done by Jeffrey Gitomer and How to Make SH*T Happen by Sean Whalen. I highly recommend both of these books, as they have offered me a ton of value. However, for this conversation, there will be no generality or ambiguity as to what in the fuck this S.H.I.T. is.

S.H.I.T. is my acronym for an easy way to remember Story, Health, Income, and Time, which are the four areas of control that determine our quality of life. It's important to understand that these are controls, like burners on a stove, that get turned up and down based on the amount of energy you apply to them. These are different from areas of focus, such as Faith, Family, Fitness, Finance, and Fun, which we will talk about later. Let's break down this acronym for a quick and dirty understanding of what this S.H.I.T really means:

S (Story): Your story is what defines you - This is the truth you are willing to admit to others and the lies that you tell yourself. Every mission or journey starts with knowing where you are right now. All of your life's experiences, whether pretty or shitty, have shaped your perspectives, beliefs, fears, and desires. Being honest about those things matter.

Your story is the face that you show to the world based on your perception of your experiences. Don't miss this point. You, as a person, are the sum of your reactions to what you have seen, heard, and learned. All of what has happened across your timeline shapes your identity, which is your inner person who influences how you show up in the world. It's the good, the bad, and the ugly, but it's yours to own. Don't shy away from reflecting on your past, acknowledging your mistakes, or celebrating your wins. They all contribute to who you are today.

H (Health): Physical and mental health is the measure of what you are capable of and how long you will be here doing it. This accounts for how you prioritize things like exercise, nutrition, meditation, and sufficient recovery. This is the area of life where we consider how much do we really love and respect ourselves.

Your health is your wealth, both physically and mentally. People who think they don't have enough time to take care of themselves should consider that taking care of themselves is the only thing that gives people more time. Super FACTS. Putting a value on the strength of your body and mind allows you to perform at your best and enjoy life to the fullest. How you eat, sleep, exercise, and manage stress can make or break your well-being. Don't neglect your self-care, and invest in your health like the valuable asset it is.

I (Income): Having a stable income with resources to fund your lifestyle is essential to a happy life. How much you produce, protect, and preserve wealth determines most of the experiences you will have in the world. Any King who cannot provide for himself and his family will, at some point, be stripped of his crown. Period.

Your income, or how you make and manage money, determines the opportunities and experiences you can afford. Whether you're an entrepreneur or an employee, you need to find ways to create value, generate income, and save and invest smartly. Money may not buy happiness, but it sure can alleviate many of life's stresses and give you the freedom to pursue your passions.

T (Time): You cannot appreciate life without respecting your own time because they are one and the same. There is no more precious resource in the world than <u>YOUR time</u>. This is measured in two parts. The first is the discipline to avoid distractions that could enslave your attention, thus stealing your time. Secondly, the choices that you make every day add joy to your life and bring happiness to others.

Your time is your life's currency. You can't buy more of it, and you can't get back what's already gone. Every second you spend on trivial or unfulfilling bullshit is a second you'll never get to use again. Respect your time by prioritizing what matters, avoiding distractions, and being intentional about how you use it. Make every moment count, and don't take tomorrow for granted.

Circumstances and other people create situations that can be totally out of our control, but that doesn't make us victims to them. The reason for this book is to highlight the powers that we do have to regulate our performance in life based on what we can control despite whatever else is going on; those controls are your S.H.I.T. (Got it!) With the definition of the acronym locked in, let's consider what these 'controls' mean for you. It's important for you to understand that each of these controls operates like knobs on the burner of a stove. Turning up the gas or electricity creates more heat, and when you have all four burners on high, your S.H.I.T. is really cooking! But where we go wrong is when we stop paying attention to the controls, and they will gradually start turning themselves down, then ultimately shut the fuck off. Period.

Soon as We *Stop Fighting* for What we <u>Do Want</u>,

what we <u>Don't Want</u> will *Automatically* Take Over

- Les Brown

This takes constant effort and a system on autopilot for us to keep this up for a lifetime. However, you will only do this when <u>your satisfaction</u> with <u>your results</u> becomes <u>your highest priority</u>.

-   Are you prioritizing your Story, your Health, your Income, and your Time like the precious resources they are?
-   Are you letting life happen to you without a plan or a purpose?
-   What are you doing each day to achieve your Dreams?

This is going to be a grind at first but its doable and required. Eric Thomas said, "You can't cheat the grind. It knows how much you've invested, and it won't give you a penny more than that." FACTS.

We will go into much more depth on the four S.H.I.T. controls in the next chapter, but we need to handle some other understandings first.

A Pawn to A KING

For the first two decades of my adulthood, I learned to be a master of making my life look like I was doing great. But we all know that salt looks like sugar from a distance. I desperately wanted someone or something to blame for all the potholes in my lawn. My reality was fucked up, and although I didn't vocalize it, I was waiting for a savior. I wanted help, and I needed help, but I just didn't have the balls to ask for it. By the way, all of this stuff happening could not be my fault, right? I labeled everything and anything as "out of my control," so that I did not have to assume full responsibility for my bad choices. Meanwhile, I was convinced that external factors were the source of all my problems. These included the government, racist white people, bad tenants, stealing employees, my wife was a bitch, my mom died too early, my dad wasn't there enough, and the list went on forever. I was trapped in a story that it was all their fault; that way of thinking made me powerless!

<u>WHOEVER IS TO BLAME IS IN CONTROL.</u>

Blame others, and they are in control.

Blame yourself, and you are in control.

When it's their fault, they must fix it.

When it's your responsibility, you can fix it.

FACTS. Consider this: What if your car was rear-ended while stopped at a traffic light? Imagine replacing the thought of how it is totally **<u>not your fault</u>** with "I should have been monitoring behind me for that." Quite possibly, you could have invested in a rear-view detection system that alerts you when a car could hit you from behind. Now, by the way, Tesla has already done it! Fast forward, Geico might pay for the damages because you were dead right, but if that accident was fatal, you would really be DEAD, right? This is the big secret to getting your life back on your terms. No reasons are good enough to keep settling for less than a life worth living. The only option is to become absolutely <u>unreasonable!</u> Meaning you are not to be fucking reasoned with. <u>No Negotiating</u> about who is responsible for everything that happens in your life; it does not matter who or what else shows up in the story.

He who accepts responsibility for EVERYTHING

can learn to control EVERYTHING;

He who Controls EVERYTHING is KING

Accepting this truth may trigger Guilt, Shame, Blame, and Anger. Nobody wants those feelings. When things go wrong, humans, by nature, create reasons and righteousness for why we are the victim. Praise God that I got tired of smelling my own shit and decided to become someone else. I was not looking for improvement or to have some degree of better. I wanted everything radically different. I wanted a new life, so I had to become a new person. Since two things, or people, cannot occupy the same space at the same time, the old mother fucker I was being had to go – permanently! At all costs. I was willing to kill off the character I was being and be reborn as a different persona. Like in reincarnation (but NOT LITERALLY DEAD). I thought long and hard about who could possibly be the greatest type of man in the world. Then, like a ton of bricks, it hit me. I was living like a peasant, and now I wanted to be a **KING**. So, I gave myself that exact title as my new identity and would not accept anything less from this man but excellence.

Historically, there are two types of kings. The royalty king gets his position from entitlement or birthright without having to do anything significant to receive it. On the other side is the Warrior King, who was required to capture his position and was required to prove his worthiness as a king. Being a Warrior King is greatness because anyone that is committed and willing to live by the code can be that man.

Most men's ego would have them believe they are worthy of the title KING because they can swing their dick around in the bank, or the bar, or the bedroom, but that's bullshit. The title 'King' is not like bro, man, dude, homeboy. Nope. Being a king is not about dominance and respect from others, but it's about service and truth. When you're a <u>true King</u>, you think differently because you are honorable, responsible, and accountable. You become a fixed point where righteousness is— like a Lighthouse. Your job is to create things, protect what you create, and ensure everything around you is blooming and thriving. That's what a KING does, but we never reach the finish line as King. Doctors and Lawyers, too, are continually in a state of practicing their craft. So, we as kings, will always be in a state of growth.

I declare that I'm King, but I'm not confessing to be perfect. For years, I shelved this very project because I thought I was not good enough. I thought, *"I'm not a minister or preacher like Eric Thomas, I'm not an expert like Tony Robbins, I'm not clean-cut like Darren Hardy. I'm a rebel. I* drink whiskey whenever I want. I'd rather watch movies than read a book. And I curse like I'm getting paid to do it. Regardless of all the balls I've dropped, what I have done for sure is got my shit together." My faith and purpose are on-point, my connection with my family is solid, my fitness is on fire, my finances are strong, and overall, my future is finally looking bright. So, despite the natural feelings of 'not being good enough,' I am KING. I believe there are millions of men just like me looking for this exact message. And it had to come from someone just like them.

Decide what you want!

Big question, have you ever asked yourself what do YOU really want? Not a generality of "to be successful" or some other cliche motivation seminar bullshit. No, I mean real specific, details galore of what you want. And... you have to want it just because you want it. If you didn't have to count the cost of it, or figure out where you find it, or whatever other sacrifice you imagine is required to have it. Just want something because you want it. Removing all the limits of practical reality and reasons why you would not be able to have it. Most people never do. We get stuck in the how before we ever consider the real what. Historically, if the limits of what people wanted were based on what they knew how to achieve, we as a species would not be remotely as evolved as we are now. We call them the crazies, the explorers, and the inventors because they desire to have something that may not exist or there is no clear path to getting to it. Such is your best life. The only people truly living their best life are the ones that just started going in a direction; that made sense and figured it out along the way, no matter what they bumped into. Because they really, really, really wanted it.

Want is a very important topic because most people prioritize what they go after in life by a different word – NEED. I need food, need shelter, need my wife, need my children, need more money, need whatever. That's all a LIE. A person only needs oxygen if they WANT to continue living. There is only a requirement of breathing if you desire to stay alive. All the proof you could want is found through historical suicide by hanging. YOU MUST WANT TO LIVE. When you choose something else and do something else, you will get something else. By understanding this concept, you will realize that you **DON'T NEED ANYTHING.** However, you can **WANT EVERYTHING.** The difference is all about power and control. When you believe that you are in control of whatever you will have, there is power for you to obtain it. If you are "needy," then you are powerless, and nobody likes a needy mother fucker. Try declaring these common statements out loud and see if they make a difference in the way you feel about the ideas:

- I want more money.
- I want to be in love with my wife.
- I want my children to adore me.
- I want my company to be successful.
- I want to take a Vacation and relax.
- I want to be fit and in shape.
- I want a Bigger house.
- I want a new Car.

- I want to have more sex.
- I want to find my purpose in life.
- I want to have a soulmate.
- I want to finish reading this book!

I lived most of my life using the word NEED instead of want in those statements. And that just sucks. Each of these statements has a result that provides satisfaction and happiness, which is what I want. And I know that if I don't want happiness and gratification, I don't have to do any of the things required to make that happen. This, too, would suck, but at least I am in control of the suck. That makes me powerful. Having your mindset in a place of "I Want" or "I Don't Want" is like being in the throne room of a King.

Once you figure out what it is that you want - Ask yourself who do you know of that has it. They could be any person in the world or even a fictional character. What you must consider is their traits, disciplines, skills, or the responsibilities that come along with having that thing. I can promise you that a person who has earned the result you are dreaming about had to become worthy enough to have it before they actually got it. Showing up at a river full of fish ready to be caught is only part of the process. The fisherman has to come with a basket big enough to hold all the fish he plans on catching, or he can fish his ass off all day, but he can only take home as much fish as can fit in the basket. Yes, he is going to need a rod, a net, some bait, and fishing skills, but with all of that, he must still be prepared to manage the haul. As a kid, I would go to a restaurant and order twice as much food as I could actually eat. My mother would say, "Boy, you gonna be sick because your eyes are bigger than your belly." My question to you is, are you even ready for the S.H.I.T. that you think you want? Is the container of who YOU are big enough to hold the dreams you have in your head?

- If you instantly became CEO of a multimillion-dollar international company, are you capable of running it?
- If the woman of your dreams was ready to commit to you for marriage and children, are you prepared to support that?
- If a once-in-a-lifetime travel opportunity with your favorite celebrity became available, could you afford to go?
- If the entire world stopped and listened to you, would you know what to say?

Without something to fight for, we are lost.

Without a reason to want something, we want anything.

Without a want of our own, we end up with nothing.

- KING SMALLS

The Bottom Line

Since the beginning of time, men have been fighting wars over food, land, resources, and women. It is easy for us to see and understand why there is conflict and competition around these things. As soon as we become aware of our balls, there is a constant struggle to have what is required and chase down what we desire. War happens when other people are in the way. Alongside the obvious, there has also been an invisible war that we are waging, which determines if we will have the most powerful resource of all, the Power of Self. **Power is the ability to control things and situations. Self-power is the ability to control situations within your own world.**

Our four controls, **Story**, **Health**, **Income**, and **Time,** are also like resources, similar to water, food, or oil. When a society loses dominance over these resources, it gets desperate and could ultimately die. The more power we have over resources (like our S.H.I.T. controls), the more power we have. No one can steal your Story, Health, Income, or Time, but if you are not controlling them, something else or someone else will! The force we use to control all of these things is our **attention**. Where attention goes, energy flows. You must understand that when someone is not paying attention, they are not in control. People are easily influenced to give up their money and time when they are distracted by either what they **want** or what they **don't**

want. If you are constantly scared of global catastrophe, you will give all your attention to the news and pay for stockpiles of end-of-the-world' supplies. If you are craving some female attention, you might spend the night in a strip club, giving away all the money you made for the week. Anything that takes our attention away from controlling our S.H.I.T. is a distraction. Everything wants your attention. The obvious things are social media, product advertisers, and your job. But what about pride, lust, greed, and fear? They want your attention too!

On the other hand, when our attention is directed toward dominating our S.H.I.T., we become focused and focus leads to maximum control. When we allow the world's distractions to scatter our attention, we reduce the energy we have to spend on our own S.H.I.T.

Sunlight scattered through glass creates light.

Sunlight focused through a laser creates power.

Light is nice, power is Godly. Focus is God's gift to getting results, and there is no greater devil in the world than distractions that steal your attention. The true source of our power is focus, and the currency of focus is attention.

The Groundwork

The War is For **Attention**,

Attention Creates **Focus**,

And Focus Creates **Power**.

The bottom line is **distractions cause you to lose power.** This book is about the war against distractions. Every moment of every single day, you have choices, decisions, and opportunities to lose that power or give it away. Even the ones you love most are unintentionally trying to steal your power. If you want to be more, do more, and have more, then you are going to need all the focus you can get.

So how do you acquire the focus required to create power predictably and on-demand every single day? It is the decision to focus on your own S.H.I.T.!

You may be interested in what's going on in the world around you, but more importantly, what's going on in *your* world? You care about the country's economy, but what's going on with your finances? You care about global health and worry about the next pandemic, but what's going on with your health? You care about celebrity relationships, statistics of divorce, and your fucking neighbors, but what's going on with your family? Years ago, I realized that it's great to be empathetic about what's going on in the world from a big-picture point of view, but I had to ask myself: What about my own life? Who is worrying about what's going on with me? My story is for people who know they have been riding a roller coaster of chaotic circumstances brought on by their own choices, and they are tired of losing. They are ready to say, *"Enough!"*

We are born to be Kings! To get laid, cool in the shade, and have all of our bills paid. No matter what has happened before, **you have the potential to do more than you're doing right now. But if you're stuck in what you know, and what you're used to doing, there won't be any significant change in your life.**

ACTION vs. DISTRACTION

This battleground is about getting results. The question is, "Am I producing an action or am I involved in a distraction?" See, a distraction could be an actual thing. You could be doing it, and it appears as an action. Understand what I'm saying. Just because I'm doing something productive, does not mean the results I will get are leading me toward my big target. You could be doing lots of good tasks that always keep you doing something that appears fruitful but all you have to show for your results is activities. That's a disease called "Busy-O-Citus"

There are lots of people who are busy. But in fact, they are busy, busy, busy, and busy being broke. They're busy being distracted. They're busy being tired, and always seem to be busy as hell. They're not actually 'getting shit done.' There's a difference when you take an action. An action moves you in the direction of real results; not into a fantasy. It is also not random busyness just to impress others. No. This is about focusing on things that get your S.H.I.T. together. See, because if you are doing, and doing, and doing, but it's just benefiting somebody else, it has nothing to do with your life.

Let's consider it for a moment. In all of the tasks that you have to get done for the day, do those things take you to the big goal you have for yourself. the thing that if you got it done changes your world. You would look back and say, "Hey, my day was successful," and if you keep having successful days like that, you will ultimately have successful weeks. And a bunch of successful weeks means successful months, and successful years, and ultimately, a successful life. You don't have to foresee every step you must take in your life, take consistent actions that move you toward your target.

This battleground is to eliminate things that are distractions, posing like they are important, but they're not. For example, you might be thinking "I've got to wash my laundry right now." So you stop what you're doing and go spend two hours at the fucking laundry mat. When maybe you could have paid somebody else to do that because it's a $30 job, and you earn $300 an hour. I don't know what you earn, but I know that you need to be able to quantify each one of those tasks to a dollar. You need to be able to quantify it to a result. Everything you do, you have to ask yourself, "Should I make this a job for someone else, or do I take this on myself? Does this take me away from my target or push me towards it."

You have to separate your actions from your distractions based on what the result is going to bring you, and if it's something that doesn't move you toward your target, even if it needs to get handled, it doesn't mean that it needs to get handled by you. You separate the actions from the distractions. You are a powerful magnet for circumstances, things, and people competing for your attention. Lots of people will bring situations and tasks to derail and distract you. Not intentionally, but they will do it because they know you are powerful. You must be able to separate your desire to be helpful. So, ask yourself, where am I taking action, and where am I being distracted every single day? That's your task for now. It's the battleground for your mind. Together, we will discover more tools for becoming focused and getting your S.H.I.T. together.

Summary: Action vs Distraction

The world is filled with noise and distractions, threatening to steal your time and focus. Winning the battle between action and distraction is a matter of discipline, commitment, and laser-focused attention. It's time to rise above the chaos and take control of your life.

Power Action Step:

- Identify distractions: List the top 5 distractions that have been sabotaging your progress. This could be anything from social media to toxic relationships or procrastination.
- Prioritize your goals: Clearly define your short-term and long-term goals. Know your priorities and stay committed to them.
- Eliminate or minimize distractions: Ruthlessly cut out or reduce the impact of distractions in your life. Set boundaries, create routines, and establish a dedicated workspace to stay focused.
- Develop a daily action plan: Create a daily schedule that aligns with your priorities and goals. Set aside specific time blocks for focused work and stick to them, no matter what.

The next four chapters are a deeper dive into each of the elements of our S.H.I.T., and we will define them as powerful controls in our lives. Be proud of yourself for making it this far. the U.S. Navy Seals are an exclusive unit because they take average men through fire until they become exceptional... Prepare to be challenged and know that you are on your way to exceptional.

CHAPTER ONE

- STORY

Defining your story requires being honest about the truths you share with others and the lies you tell yourself. It rarely is the entire truth because it is made up by the perception of the person who created the story! This is like a report on the TV news that has been filtered through emotions, personal trauma, religion, memories, cultural understandings, and world views of the newscaster. To get the truth from a story, you must separate the facts from the feelings. Separate what actually is from what you feel that it is. Separate what actually happened from what you believe or wished happened. Separate what they actually said from what you think they meant. This is how you break apart reality from fantasy. You must find the facts. When your mind is focused, so are the words you speak.

You'll get there by removing anything that is a fact. There's a story about Michelangelo, the gifted sculptor of the iconic statue of David. He was asked how he was able to create David from that gigantic slab of marble. He responded something like, "I didn't create David. He was already in the marble. All I had to do was remove everything that wasn't David."

There is always a story, and then there is the real story. Real means actual, factual, measurable truth. This is the stuff that reality is made of, but most of us were not taught to require this as a cornerstone for life. And if you are currently operating the way I was, you've been "faking the funk," like my daddy used to say. A man behind a facade. I know this because when my truth was revealed, it was like my entire world was chocolate-covered dog crap. If you are wasting time, energy, and money to make people think your situation is different than it really is - that shit must change right now.

When you decide what results you want, you will **no longer** settle. you must declare what you will **no longer** tolerate in your life. I do not tolerate lying or being lied to in my life, PERIOD. You must draw a line in the sand for what is non-negotiable. Then you must decide what you are willing to sacrifice to have the new life you want. I sacrificed my pride and my ego, which may make me vulnerable to every possible criticism and judgment from people. Once this is clearly identified, it's time to ask yourself, "so where am I now?"

When you look at a map, the first thing you need to know is **where you are at**. No matter how expensive of a navigation system you have, if it can't find where you are AT

NOW, it will never be able to take you where you want to go. The problem with most people in getting where they're going is they decide on these altruistic, powerful, imaginative goals and things they see other people having. They decide that they want to go in that direction, but there is no way they can ever get there, because they never admit the truth about where they are AT NOW. That comes from telling the truth, and it comes from having the integrity of your word.

When I say integrity, I'm talking about the strength of your word. When you say that you're going to get some shit done, do you actually do it? Are you negotiable? Are you reasonable? Simply meaning do you allow yourself to make excuses that you nicely labeled as reasons? Do You make reasons that get you out of actually doing the shit that you say you're going to do, or do you have non-negotiable integrity in your word? Are your commitments so rock solid, that when you say something to people who know you, they have absolutely no doubt it's getting done? Or do they expect to hear some 'reasonable' (like bullshit) story for why you could not do what was required? My grandmother used to say, "Now, that's where the rubber meets the road boy."

When I knew I was behind on bills, I relied on some super evasive strategies to avoid conversations about money. I developed a sophisticated cat-and-mouse game with the *"Repo Man"* AKA 'Scofflaw Towing' in New York City. Make no mistake; there's a real racket being run that allows certain people to profit off of broke people. If you don't have the money to pay the ticket, you damn sure don't have the money to pay all the late fees and fines. My little shitty choices of where I parked my car cost me big. By the time I paid the initial tickets, towing fee, impound fees, transportation, all that bullshit adds up to thousands of dollars. On top of that, my car was scratched up and crazy mistreated in the dirty ass tow yard. And that was my pattern frequently. Get a ticket, not pay the ticket, get towed, incur fines, and pay out the ass to get my car back. Friends of mine started to recognize this and would check me like, "Smalls, why don't you just pay your tickets, man?" The answer was I didn't respect the value of my credit with the law, and therefore my credit was shot. I treated everything like this. I would say im going to pay my ticket but fail to do it. If you had a credit score for honoring your word, what would it say about you? Would it be a 500 or a 600, or an 800? Based on all the agreements you have made in the past and every time you followed through with what you said, do you get shit done? Are you really accomplishing what you say you are going to do, or just making empty promises waiting to get your ass towed?

When we decide, without question, shit must get done, we actually get shit done. I am deliberate about using the word decide because it means something quite different than what many people understand it to be. Most of us think that deciding is the same as making a choice, but they have very different meanings. Making a choice is a flexible and changeable thing. For example, if you were on your way to a Chinese food restaurant when you smelled some bangin' pizza and chose to go for that instead, would you have beef with the Chinese restaurant? Hell No. There was no obligation to eat from that restaurant because your choice had no agreement with them. However, a decision is a choice that is backed by a commitment, which is an agreement you must honor. This is a crossroads. That means there is no way out, and you figuratively have to burn the boats. The bridge is blown, and you can't go backward. Going forward you must do whatever your decision calls for until you have a new agreement! Yes, that is possible. If your circumstances change and you decide something different, you can make a change to a decision, but it must be clearly replaced by a new agreement. When you make the commitment of your word so important that your life is as important as the integrity of your word, you become your word! From this point, you will do the things you say, and that's when you start getting things in your life done differently. This is a crucial factor for getting your S.H.I.T. together.

When I was a kid, we had a saying called "word is born." Basically, word is born means that I gave birth to my word, and my honor and reputation is behind whatever I'm saying. As kids we would also grab our balls when we made the declaration, which meant that If I break my word, then I am breaking my balls. And, since I always liked my balls... You get the picture. So, I'm going to tell you, if you like your balls, don't break your word. Be honest and true to yourself. You may have made mistakes in the past. We all did. We all continue to do it, but what if you made your word the most important thing that you had? When I say something, I want people to believe it like they saw it with their own eyes. When the truth of your mouth, becomes gospel, you can move people without touching them. At that point, you have arrived. That's the true power of your word.

The integrity of your word is paramount to getting your S.H.I.T. together. That's where we start. You have to begin with the truth to end in reality. When you can be honest about where you are, then you can determine if you have the sacrifice, the capability, and the willingness to go where your heart wants you to go. And if you can't say it, mean it, and actually do it without question, then that is the type of S.H.I.T. that just doesn't flush.

Integrity

We grew up with a saying in my neighborhood that was powerful and universally accepted – "Word is bond." It was a verbal contract that what we just said was "facts" or whatever we were planning to do, was guaranteed. Even for kids too young to see over the counter in the bodega without tippy toeing, we knew how real this was. Your word is your sworn oath that what you say is the truth. We would sign contracts of conversation with "that's on my word and my balls." Therefore, if I'm lying or breaking my word, it's just like sacrificing my balls; nobody wants to lose their balls. Another way you could think about this came to me from Landmark Education's The Forum. This was a powerful training series that gave me a real gut check on keeping my word. The message was, "You are your word, and your word is who you are." Period. The measurement of how you honor your word is **integrity**. This is the strength of the fabric of your word. When you say that you're going to get a project done, do you actually do it, or do you negotiate with yourself and make excuses that will get you out of getting the project done? Are you focused? Does your word mean so much that you hold yourself accountable without question? The ability for you to be honest with others and yourself is your story, PERIOD.

Men with good intentions make promises,

Men with Good Character Keep Promises,

you can love them both,

But you only Respect one of them!

You have to be 100% honest about what's going on in your life. I want you to be able to say out loud what you truly feel. When you are real as fuck, you will acknowledge these feelings and be moved to take meaningful action. However, suppose you only operated based on feelings? In that case, you would probably end up in a world of craziness because feelings can be as unpredictable as the weather. However, they are important and valuable because they are the force that gets us to take action. Think about this: anytime you did anything, you were compelled to do it because of a feeling. Either happy, hungry, horny, or whatever other desire drove you to do it. You must learn to use these feelings as a tool without suppressing them. We must fully express ourselves, take action, then move forward. When I finally realized that it was okay for me to express my feelings, without worrying about what society says, I became free. When I chose not to be docile and passive, I became dominant and confident. This was like **Liberation from emotional constipation.** I began to share my story more clearly and honestly, focusing on what mattered most in a way that gave me freedom. For years, I used drinking as my scapegoat to be reckless with a built-in excuse for stupid ass behavior. Now, I don't need to be drunk to say what is on my mind because my beliefs and feelings are my authenticity. The other way of being was a waste of focus and power.

If your STORY is the seed for growing a real life, then authenticity is the soil. I had the pleasure of being in a training room with the great Les Brown, where he said, "Everyone is born Unique, but most of us die as Copies," Super Facts. We, humans, are like the fingerprints of God, connected to the same source, but each one is different in some kind of way. Despite such a blessing of being special, our drive for social approval, and fear of being ridiculed, we sacrifice our individualism for the safety of acceptance.

Herd animals eat shit. Facts. Wildebeests travel as the largest herd groups in the world across the plains of Africa because there is safety in just being a look-alike in the large crowd. They bunch up together, grazing and shitting through the same grasslands. Imagine One hundred thousand animals pissing, shitting, and eating in the same area. This is their life because survival depends on staying as close to the middle of the pile as possible and not drawing any attention to themselves. The idea is to blend within the blur. In the distance, lions and wolves in small packs, each with individual talents and jobs for the hunt, prey on the group. The universal strategy is to search for a stray or any sign of difference they consider as a weakness for easy pickings. When they strike and the prize is captured, the first and best choice of meat is taken in order of dominance and leadership; The King eats first. The focus here is not predator and prey but what they will eat based on their association with the tribe. Where are you at? Are you living as just another dude in the crowd, or a spectator in the stands talking crap about the players on the field? Or are you taking chances, hunting with the elite, and following your dreams? I can guarantee that the moment your story becomes rooted in the authentic version of yourself, you will never go back to eating shit with the herd again. Unshackled by not giving a flying fuck what other people think about your story, you will hunt down incredible trophies, big game goals and devour the best experiences this world has to offer.

No More Lies

Stop Lying and Tell the Truth sounds like a redundant statement, but they are two completely separate ideas. To Lie is an act of commission, where you blatantly say something that you know ain't true. Not telling the truth is an act of omission, where you know something that is relevant and consequential, but you don't say it to manipulate the outcome directly. The insidious thing about this is that many people believe they cannot do anything wrong by just keeping their mouths shut. However, choosing not to do or say something is an action; all actions have effects. FACTS. Both of these acts have their place in the world as a weapon to get what you want or as a shield to protect you from something that you don't want. However, most of the time, we use them as selfish manipulation, which is wicked and creates a false reality.

If I had a brick for every lie that I've told, I could build a got damn skyscraper! Lies create walls that keep other people from seeing the truth, but after a while, we can no longer see the truth ourselves. We get trapped in a maze of walls that contort the way we see ourselves and the world we are living in. They are a double-edged sword that cuts them and us. Coming to the point that I decided my life had to change began with the realization I was living in a fantasy world. A maze of fake stories I would have friends and family believe so that my image of being the mother fucking man was preserved. Buying champagne in the club with mortgage money is a lie, even if you don't open your mouth. Strategically posting pictures of your wife and kids on social media but not coming home three or four nights a week is a fucking lie. And the more that I found ways to create this deception for others the more I started to believe the bullshit I was sitting in smelled like roses. The answer I found to change my life was not some powerful set of actions to do, but instead was the toughest question I had to ask myself. Who am I being?

KRS ONE receiving Lifetime Achievement Award

Who Are You Being

I had the pleasure of sharing the stage and spending time with one of the greatest philosophers and historians of our lifetime, the Teacha KRS ONE. If you don't know who he is, that is a travesty, and it needs to be rectified right now. I hosted KRS as the guest speaker for the first Rise of the Black Warrior event, and I began to study some of his thoughts on organized religion and the history of it. Without going too deep into that conversation, our values determine how we act and treat others, and values start with our beliefs. One of the most beautiful things about our mind is how it creates faith based on whatever we truly believe. Here is what I believe: God is supreme, the spirit of all-knowing that responds to my prayers, I believe he is there and continues to show up for me. My faith that God exists is unwavering because there is no other possible explanation for the unmerited blessings and favor I have received when I am connected to him. The Universe is the force that brings things from the spirit into our world, Like the law of attraction and Karma. I believe God has created laws in this world that just work and are irrefutable when you test them over time. Lastly, Nature is the force that responds to the physical rules of this world, Like gravity and the circle of life. These are the cause-and-effect laws that science can prove didn't just pop out of nowhere. KRS coins this with the analogy G.U.N. (God, Universe, Nature). This is NOT my religion, it's just a simple way of explaining to others what makes most sense to me. Furthermore, I do not claim any religion, but I share the value of my relationship with the spirit of God that I know is with me.

There are hundreds of documented and recognized religions around the world, with believers who are absolutely positively sure that their religion is the right one! We all want to be right. Throughout history, wars have been fought, and countless people have died because people disagreed about who or what God is, even what the rules are for living on this shared space rock. However, I believe that it can all be boiled down to nature's most basic agreement:

The Golden Rule. "Treat others as you would have them treat you." And that is the guiding principle for my life. But to make it more applicable to my personal growth, and living a life I can be proud of, I expanded it to:

"**BE** unto others as I would have them **BE** unto me."

The truth is, we are Human **BEINGS**,

not Human **Doings**.

- By becoming the person that I would like to be married to, I became a great husband.
- By becoming a person, I would like to do business with, I became a great entrepreneur.
- By becoming the person, I would respect as a healthy role model, I became a physically fit athlete.
- By becoming a man, I thought my creator would be proud of, I became an honest person.

My choice was to focus on how I showed up in the world toward others as I would want for myself. And by observing this one rule of nature every being in the world can respect and appreciate that. Every living thing desires to be treated with respect, care, and honesty. That is my religion. The term "religious" can be defined as rituals or practices honored with consistency and regularity. Therefore, when I religiously work on becoming the person that I want to be around in my life, I am BEING worthy of this gift of life. What more could anyone else need to know?

THE 6 HUMAN NEEDS

I rarely use the word need because it's a weak expression for wanting something, whereas simply saying WANT is powerful. However, for the sake of this discussion, I am going to share a lesson on the nature of people. I have learned in the same way, that I learned it so that you can dive deeper into the core concerns of human beings, which are the things we want and don't want. Based on this, you may better choose who you will become in your story.

Step 1: Decoding the Six Human Needs

I discovered these six human needs from live training with the great Tony Robbins many years ago, and even after a decade of reviewing and challenging them, they still hold true. I would like you to consider them in a specific context for discovering who you BE.

- Certainty: Craving safety, comfort, and predictability.
- Variety: Thirsting for challenges, change, and thrill.
- Significance: Yearning to feel special, important, and respected.
- Love/Connection: Desiring deep connections and feeling cherished.
- Growth: Seeking personal evolution, knowledge, and expansion.

- Contribution: Wanting to give back, assist others, and make a deposit into the universe.

We all have these needs, but their prominence varies. Think of these needs as character traits that you can resonate with. For example, Certainty is a need for people that like to feel safe and secure. These are people that look ten times before crossing the street, only invest in things that have been around for a hundred years and prefer to take the same route back and forth to work each day. These people are not excited about big changes and will avoid people who are volatile in their choices. Understanding that if this is the most important thing to you from the six needs, you will be most happy when your decisions about Business, relationships, and fun are in alignment with this. Therefore, if a friend booked you a two-week river adventure vacation staying in a tent outdoors in the mountains of Chile, that asshole is not really your friend.

Step 2: Scrutinizing and Prioritizing Your Needs

Once you've got a grip on these needs, it's time to scrutinize and rank them. This calls for brutal honesty and introspection. Ask yourself, "Which of these needs are non-negotiable? Which ones drive my actions, decisions, and emotions?"

Identify the top three needs that hit home for you. You may value certainty, love/connection, and growth above all. Or significance, variety, and contribution are what get you out of bed in the morning. There's no right or wrong here - only what rings true for you.

Step 3: Living Your Truth

With your top three needs in clear sight, the final leg of this journey is to align your life with these needs. This means making conscious choices that satisfy these needs.

If growth ranks high on your list, you might take on a challenging project, learn a new skill, or invest in personal development. If love/connection resonates with you, you might focus on nurturing relationships, spending quality time with loved ones, or volunteering.

By aligning your life with your top human needs, you won't just discover your authentic self but also engineer a life that brings you joy, satisfaction, and fulfillment.

To wrap it up, getting a handle on your human needs is like turning on a spotlight on your authentic self. By scrutinizing and ranking these needs, you can uncover profound truths about who you are and what makes you tick. By living a life that aligns with these needs, you can make choices that truly reflect your authentic self. Self-discovery requires honesty and a path to get there. This process won't happen overnight, it's a journey that is just as valuable as the destination. Powerful S.H.I.T.

The Bottom Line

Owning your story is the start. Every high and low, is part of the journey, and we must acknowledge and respect these aspects regardless of how they make you feel. There's no hiding or pretending. the first step to growth is owning it. We must first be honest with ourselves before we can be truthful with others. Our real story is based on the willingness to stop lying to ourselves and tell the truth with our words and actions to others. We must tap into our feelings and become fully self-expressed about what matters to us. However, we rewrite our story by coming to grips with reality and removing emotion and feelings from the facts. Feelings are important, but they cloud our understanding of the unfiltered truth. Our decisions must be grounded in reality.

Integrity is everything. If you can't keep your word, you've got nothing. This isn't a game, and it's not about how others perceive you. It's about self-respect and living with honor. No excuses, no shortcuts. Real strength means sticking to your word even when it's tough, even when no one's watching.

We are human beings, not human doings. We must strive to become the person that we want to be around, deserving of respect and admiration. Be the change and the partner we would desire, the businessperson we would respect, the role model we would admire, and be the honest man our creator would be proud of.

To become that person, we discover our true nature through the six human needs. Certainty, variety, significance, love/connection, growth, and contribution – find out what drives us. What matters. Know those needs, align life with them, and make choices that fulfill them. This is the way to build a life that mirrors the true self.

So, this is it, the direction toward a life you will be proud of: Own the story, live with integrity, speak the truth, BE the desired person, and align life with your needs. It's simple, and it's the only way to an authentic, real life. FACTS.

REALITY vs. FANTASY

When someone that weighs 200 lbs. states that they are fat, they could believe that is a fact. However, the only fact is that they weigh 200 lbs., and their perception of themselves is that they are fat. The scale creates an undeniable truth that stands alone and doesn't require any belief about it. However, the story that they are fat does. If the person receiving that conversation weighs 400 pounds, they might disagree and say, "No, You're not fat, I'm fat." So either nobody is fat, or somebody is playing Mr. please don't feel bad. All of this chatter is relative to who's interpreting the information, and truthfully none of this bullshit is facts. So that makes all of it a big fat story. A fact could be a certain weight for a specific height is considered overweight based on a specific guideline. The guideline is a defined, measurable thing that becomes a fact. That becomes a reality. Now, on the other hand, someone thinking, "Hey, I'm in good shape," must answer the question, what is good shape? Is it measurable? Can I determine the truth based on how you see it? What is being in shape to you? Maybe I'm in shape, and you're not, or vice versa. Either way, it's all perspective and none of it fact; therefore, it's fantasy.

Perspective changes what we do about things in our lives. Consider how you see the S.H.I.T. controls of your life. You may be thinking, "Hey, I've got my S.H.I.T. together." But in truth, it's just a fantasy. It's a story that you have built up to make your ego feel good, about how others perceive your success in a particular area of life. So, what do you believe in your faith? Was that the religion you chose, or did someone else give you their religion, and you accepted it? Are you on purpose for what you should be doing with your life, or did your parents tell you to be a doctor or a lawyer or a contractor or a policeman, and you just followed that? Let's ask around your family what's real versus a fantasy around your relationship with your wife and your kids. Is it true that you are fully connected and that they can testify that you are connected to them, and they believe that? Have you verified with them that you have a good connection with your family, with your wife, and with your children? Or is it something that you believe, and you're living in this fantasy that it's all good and your stuff is handled at home? See, I was living in that fantasy for years. I was living in this fantasy that I was going to be okay with my family, and I didn't really have to do anything else with them as long as I provided for them. As long as I keep providing money and they have a place, and everything's good, then my S.H.I.T. is handled.

Until I realized that I was on the edge of divorce. Me and my wife would go months on end without sex, totally disconnected because we were operating like roommates. How is your situation with your person? How's your relationship with your children? Are you connected to them? There was a time in my life when I didn't even know what my kids were allergic to, I didn't know what they liked, I didn't know what their favorite colors were. Because it was a fantasy to me that I believed that I had my S.H.I.T. handled. Once you put reality in, I could see that it wasn't true. What about your area of fitness, your body? Have you been to the doctor to have them actually bring into reality what your numbers are? The reality of that? Or do you just believe that you're okay because you're not feeling sick right now? What's the reality of that?

What are you doing every day to contribute to the improvement of your body? Are you living in a fantasy that,

"I'm okay, and I'm healthy, and that I'll live long, and that everything's all right." What about your finances? Reality versus the fantasy of your money? Do you make enough money for the money that goes out? Have you ever made a budget and said, "Hey, listen, this is how much I'm spending. I see all my calculations. I spent this, this, this, and this. I spent $10,000 this month, but I only generated five. I'm on a decline". What's reality versus fantasy? Have I actually looked at it? It's separated from what I believe it might be, versus what it actually is!

What are you doing for others in this world?

- What are you doing for your family's future?
- What if tomorrow you are not here, what happens to them?
- Have you set up enough insurance and a plan for them?
- Have you verified that your assets are secured and safe?
- Have you created generational lessons as a legacy of knowledge for your children?
- Do you have journals, books, video recordings or something to help accelerate them forward based on your experiences?
- ...Or do you believe you've done enough, and they should be okay?

You've got to separate the fantasy from the reality. And when you do that, you have a <u>REAL WORLD</u>. You will remove the story and those things that are not real, your feelings, your stories, your emotions, and you will only have the truth of what is happening in your world and the battleground for your mind be evident. Now, you've got your S.H.I.T. to think about. Create your journal entry. Where in your world are you operating in reality, and where are you operating in fantasy? The battleground begins. It starts now.

Summary: Reality vs Fantasy

Realize this: you've been trapped in a world where reality and fantasy are constantly at war. Your dreams and aspirations are held hostage by the lies you tell yourself. It's time to break free and face the truth. Embrace reality and use it as the foundation for your wildest dreams. Only then, can you truly become unstoppable.

Power Action Step:

- Confront your fantasies: Write down the unrealistic expectations and false beliefs that have been holding you back. Be brutally honest with yourself.

- Embrace your reality: Acknowledge your current situation and accept the truth of where you are right now. Own your mistakes and setbacks while appreciating the lessons they've taught you.

- Set ambitious but achievable goals: Use your newfound clarity to set goals that are grounded in reality but still push you to reach for the stars. Remember, it's not about achieving perfection but growth.

- Take relentless action: Pursue your goals with unwavering determination and adapt to any obstacles that come your way. Stay grounded in reality while relentlessly chasing your dreams.

CHAPTER TWO

- HEALTH

I want to be really clear about something. Your overall health is a combination of physical, mental, and emotional. They all have to be aligned. We are spiritual creatures having a physical experience (and that is so deep it could be a topic for a book by itself). Our emotions influence our mind, which drives the actions that we take. This is why we must be healthy in each of these areas. I believe the most critical of them all lies with the mind, because when it goes, we go. As men, we don't hear this enough–mental health is an important part of your overall wellness. If you had a broken foot, you'd see a doctor and get it fixed. You'd at least try to be healthy again. The same goes for broken thoughts and unsettled emotions. On a regular basis, we all could use the benefit of a counselor, or when it becomes serious, professional medical treatment. And FYI, you cannot do mental surgery on yourself! If you never had access to a mirror, how would you know what you look like? That is exactly why we must have a tribe and accountability, a coalition of people around us. Our mental health is gauged by the reflection of how we treat and act with people around us. That's really it.

King – the choices you make today define your legacy. What you put in your body and how you move it ain't just something to brush off. They have consequences, and they matter. Big time. Let's keep it 100, and I'm gonna lay it out for you, so there's no uncertainty.

The Fuel

Your body is your machine, and the food you consume is your fuel. That fast food you're eating is like putting mud in your gas tank. McDonald's has indirectly killed more people than cancer! Here are some stone-cold FACTS: the CDC says poor nutrition is a big player in diseases like heart disease, type 2 diabetes, obesity, and some cancers. If you're not worried, you should be. Check this out – a study published in JAMA Internal Medicine found that diets loaded with processed foods increase your risk of an early death by 30%. No joke – that trash is putting an expiration date on your life. If that ain't enough, listen to this: according to the World Heart Federation, an unhealthy diet contributes to about 80% of premature heart disease. FYI, your heart is like very important!

Don't get ridiculous and jump on some unsustainable crash diet you have seen on Instagram. There is no need for some bougie diet or gourmet prepackaged meals (unless that works for you and you're into that). Make a conscious choice to put your health and your future first. Every time you put something in your mouth, say what it is out loud, and if what it is sounds like something that God would be proud of you for eating, then eat it. If not, dump it.

Get Moving

Now, let's talk about getting your body in motion. Before we get going, don't allow your brain to start generating excuses about time, work, an injury, or any other bullshit. If you've got time to chill on the couch scrolling through your phone, you've got time to move. No more excuses.

You want more FACTS? Inactivity is a silent assassin. The National Institute on Aging says that not moving is a major risk factor for heart disease, obesity, and even depression. And if you think lounging around ain't a big deal, think again. A study from the Journal of the American Heart Association shows that sitting for long periods without moving bumps up the risk of an early death by 22%. You're not just sitting – you're giving away years of your life. Listen to this: a study published in The Lancet found that physical inactivity is responsible for more than 5 million deaths worldwide each year. That's no joke – sitting around can be lethal. And one more for you: the National Center for Biotechnology Information reports that regular exercise reduces the risk of chronic diseases like heart disease, diabetes, and obesity by up to 50%. That's half the risk, just by moving your body.

You don't have to be a pro athlete or a fitness freak. Find something that gets you going and that you enjoy. Walk, run, bike, swim, dance – it doesn't matter. Get your heart pumping and break a sweat. Aim for 150 minutes of moderate exercise every week. You can spare 30 minutes a day, five days a week. No doubt.

The bottom line, King, is that you have the power to shape your destiny. Being healthy means you can do more, be more, and live more. You can take care of your family, be a role model for your kids, and leave a legacy that stands the test of time. You deserve a long, healthy, and fulfilling life, and it all comes down to the choices you make today.

Let me tell you about another battle that's waged in the lives of many men: vices. You know what I'm talking about – smoking, excessive drinking, gambling without limits, and unprotected sex with random women are just a few vices we succumb to. We all got our weaknesses, and I damn sure got mine, but it's time to consider how these things are chipping away at your health, your relationships, your money, and your very life.

I'm gonna lay down some facts. First off, smoking. You know it's bad, right? Well, let me tell you just how bad. In the United States alone, smoking accounts for nearly 500,000 deaths every single year. It increases your risk for heart disease, stroke, and lung cancer. If you're puffing away, you're playing Russian roulette with your life.

And let's talk about drinking. A little bit every now and then, sure, but excessive drinking? Nah, that's where you make the worst decisions and end up with the most regrets. According to the CDC, excessive drinking leads to approximately 95,000 deaths in the United States annually. It can cause liver disease, high blood pressure, and increase your risk of cancer. Let me keep it on the "I" for this one. I have been so drunk that I left my friends at a club and woke up the next day under the back of a truck in a parking lot. This is one instance of countless that I could fill a book of shame about to account for excessive drinking. But also, what most people who are not heavy drinkers don't realize is that alcohol is mostly sugar. Too much sugar has a list as long as my arm of ways it will kill you. So, real talk if you're hitting the bottle hard, it's time to pump the brakes.

Now, gambling. Look, there's nothing wrong with enjoying a little Vegas now and then, but if you're going overboard, you're playing with fire in gasoline draws. The problem is gambling can devastate your finances, strain your relationships, and leave you in a place you don't want to be.

And the stats are staggering. Up to 2% of the U.S. population struggles with gambling addiction. That's millions of people, and if you're one of them, it's time to seek help.

And you can't forget about unprotected sex with different women. Let me keep it real with you: it's more dangerous than men wanna imagine. According to the CDC, nearly 20 million new sexually transmitted infections occur in the United States each year. And get this: about half of these occur in people aged 15 to 24. If you're out there doing your thing without protection, you're rolling the dice with your balls and could bring something home that you can't take back. Don't be that guy.

Look, I get it. Life has got its pleasures and its temptations, but as a king, you are required to make sacrifices worthy of righteous results. Not dying in a hospital because of a preventable illness is worthy of that. You deserve a life worth living. These vices they're nothing more than shackles holding you back from your full potential. It's time to break them. Get help if you need it, make better choices, and become the man you would be proud of

A Healthy Mind

Controlling our feelings and desires is what makes us healthy. Self-control and discipline of our emotions determine how we take care of ourselves.

My best friend in high school was Shane Tate, a smart, outgoing, handsome kid who could have been successful in any profession that he chose. Yet, the one thing he never should've been was an inmate. As a teen, Post High School, he found himself in a violent situation where he murdered someone. Shane wasn't an evil person or meant to become a killer. He got caught up in the streets, which eventually contaminated too many of his decisions. With actions that occurred in a matter of seconds, his life was changed forever. My friend was hit with a sentence of 20 years to life, ultimately serving 22 years in New York State prison before being returned to us. During his incarceration, we spent many years talking about his regret and the new person he had become. However, every time we hung up the phone, he was still in prison. Understanding the wickedness of his decision and fully accepting responsibility did not instantaneously change the results.

Today, we are living with the residual effects of yesterday's decisions and actions. You may not like the hands you are playing for a while, but you don't get a new hand until you've completely played out the results of the last deal.

Here is how your story plays a part in your health. When most people tell a story, they generate a blend of facts, happenings, interpretations, perspectives, feelings, and desires. No matter how much we may want our stories to change through the injection of feelings or perspectives, the facts will always remain. For example, I could say I was shopping in a store, and when I was leaving, a security guard requested to inspect my bag. Or I could rephrase that into a story such as, I was minding my own business just shopping in a store when I was accosted by a racist security guard practically accusing me of stealing. Do you see the difference? One story is just the facts. The second introduces emotions and speculation. You decide how much of each emotion is involved with your story through perspective. Not dealing with the facts and living in a story causes us to raise our anxiety, blood pleasure, and frustration. All three of which are unhealthy.

I'm not saying to hide your emotions or not deal with them. You'll end up with repressed anger and eventually have to deal with it in counseling, divorce court, prison, or developing some stress-related disease. However, anger is a valid emotion, one that doesn't always have to be negative or harmful. It can be just the right fuel you need to make big decisions that make changes in your life as well. When you get pissed off to the breaking point from being broke, busted, and disgusted, that's the perfect energy you need to make change. Learning to use this force constructively is a useful life skill, especially for men, because we are hardwired to build or break things when we get emotional.

Modern society conditions young men to suppress their feelings. We're conditioned to believe we should not show our feelings because they make us look weak or feminine. I grew up in the era of, "Don't you cry, boy, or I'll give you something to cry about!" Why didn't my sister get that speech? I am sure I deserved most of the ass-whooping I received prior to hearing that phrase. However, I didn't deserve to be neutered. Even if it's belting out a scream from the pain, I should've had the ability to express myself. Do you see how the cycle starts early? We bottled up the truth of our emotions for most of our lives, starting with small seeds like:

- Take it like a man.
- Keep it to yourself.
- Don't be so loud/excited.
- Stop playing so rough.
- Just get over it.
- Why are you crying about that?
- Kids need to be seen, not heard.

Even though we're expected to suppress our feelings, at the same time, we're expected to make things happen. We just get it done without acknowledging how we feel about the pain, trauma, stress, and fear in our lives. Making money, contributing to the household, and being a reliable partner. Even if you don't talk about it, nothing can get done without your feelings. Even right now. If you didn't have a certain feeling about what I'm saying here, you would not continue to be reading this. You would not have taken action to read any of what I'm saying.

Without positive examples of how to connect with and live our lives in a way that allows feeling to be managed by rational thinking, a lot of men are out here like ticking time bombs. Just about anything can set you off because you're a powder keg of suppressed emotions. Feelings are what cause us as men to do things that we do. It is our feelings that fuel us. It is the energy around us. We cannot suppress it. Fear, pain, anger, and frustration are all valuable energies that contribute to the foundation of your Story. We produce new facts based on that energy. But you have to be willing and open to connect with your feelings. I'm telling you this because if you want to evolve as a man, you are going to have to share feelings. This is a safe space to do that. Sharing is healthy, so let it out, KING!

The Bottom Line

You only get one machine. I have friends who spend more time and focus on caring for their car than they do their own bodies. People abuse themselves by putting garbage, food, excessive alcohol, and smoke into their bodies. If you worked your whole life for a sportscar, would you put the lowest quality gas into it that you could find? NO. So, what are you feeding your machine? And McDonald's is not food, by the way. If you're not exercising your mind by challenging yourself to think every day and creating new problems to solve, you will eventually stop knowing how to solve problems. Anything you don't use, you will lose. Many people think that once you have wealth and prestige, all of your problems will go away. Mike Tyson once said, "If you think having money makes you happy, you never had a lot of money before." How true this must be to an ultra-rich person lying on their death bed wishing for nothing more than good health and more time. Neglecting your body and your overall health can take away the priceless possibilities that we take for granted until they are gone.

DANGER vs. FEAR

There are many forces in this world. however, I want consider one above all that stops progress more than any other; that is fear. The fear that something could embarrass or hurt you could paralyze a man from taking required action. And as we know, actions are the things that produce results. And you can't get your S.H.I.T. together without taking massive action. So, let's determine and define the fact that there are reasons why people will either take an action or not. In the movie, *After earth*, featuring Will Smith and his real life son, Jaden, there was an absolutely powerful line that defines danger and fear in clear way.

Health

As his son was alone in the woods, on the verge of panic and terror from some deadly alien creature he said, "Son, danger is real, but fear is a choice." Although the environment was very hostile and the boy was scared, he explained the lesson of a lifetime. He said "danger is very real because there are things out there that could kill you, but fear is a choice because you get to choose to be afraid or not. Despite what could happen when I am faced with a situation, I must choose to do something about it or lose by default to the possibility of something that might never happen. those who act despite of dangers, create the possibility of results. But those who are fearful and do nothing are guaranteed to get no results. So am I telling you to ignore common sense? Absolutely not. There are things to be concerned about that are really fucking dangerous, and you should stay clear of them. However, most instances when we come in contact with fear, we are not in the face of real emanant danger, it is only a vision in our mind of something terrible that might happen in the future. We imagine how bad this experience could be, so we choose to be afraid.

The word 'abuse' means to abnormally or improperly use something. Fear is an abuse of your imagination. Your imagination is a creative energy force. It is a force that is used to build and create. You abuse your imagination by being in fear. Because you will create stories around it, and when your fear takes over you, it will cause you to stop taking action. Now, never forget that there are dangers. Real dangers. S.H.I.T. that could hurt you. So, you prepare for those things, and you assign time, and you get energy around preparing and making sure that your family is protected, that you are protected, that your body is protected, that your future is protected, that your businesses are all protected from real life dangers. But you cannot live in a space of fear by allowing your imagination to tell you stories about what could happen. By what you saw happen to someone else.

Danger versus fear is a battleground. So, we're going to get our S.H.I.T. together here, **TOGETHER**. Create an entry in your journal, listing experiences where you were paralyzed, to develop an understanding of when you have been faced with real danger, or traumatized because of fear? Ask yourself, where are the real dangers, and what things are you just afraid of?

You have to decide: are you going to choose fear when your imagination creates a story of doom that has not happened yet? Are you going to keep moving knowing that action in the face of danger is the only possibility for a better position. This is a battleground, and you are required to solve for those things that are really dangerous and manage the actions required while recognizing the fears and getting rid of them. Because they are paralyzing you and stopping you from getting to your real results. This battleground is in your mind, and It's time to go to war for control of your thoughts... NOW.

Summary: Danger vs. Fear

On the battlefield of life, one of the fiercest struggles you'll face is between danger and fear. Danger is real, but fear is a self-imposed cage that holds you back from unleashing your true potential. It's time to break free from the chains of fear and rise above the challenges that life throws at you.

Power Action Step:

- Confront your fears: Get your journal and start listing out your fears, no matter how big or small. Recognize the difference between genuine dangers and irrational fears that are holding you back.

- Create a plan of action: For each fear, develop a strategy to conquer it. It might involve education, seeking support, or simply diving into the unknown. Having a plan in place will give you the confidence to face your fears head-on.

- Embrace the discomfort: Fear feeds on your comfort zone. Challenge yourself to step out of it and embrace the discomfort that comes with growth. Understand that facing your fears is a crucial part of becoming the person you're meant to be.

- Reflect and celebrate: As you face and conquer your fears, document your journey in your journal. Acknowledge your progress, celebrate your victories, and learn from the setbacks.
- It's time to rise above the paralyzing grip of fear and embrace the power within you. You're a warrior, and no challenge is too great for you to conquer. Face your fears, seize the day, and let nothing stand in your way.

CHAPTER THREE

- INCOME

This was the hardest subject in our S.H.I.T. list for me to deal with because this is the area of life that was most screwed up. Income is your ability to generate, produce, protect, and preserve a lifestyle that you set for yourself. As a man, if you can't feed yourself, then you can't lead yourself! Not to mention having cool things like clothing, transportation, and a roof over your head. Without a solid stream of money, a man will experience the suffering of poverty. The clearest understanding, I have come across in regard to how much money a person makes is: **A man earns in direct proportion to the magnitude of the problems that he solves.** A man that takes on big-ass problems that affect lots of people makes big-ass checks and, alternatively, vice versa. Also, income potential is evaluated by how rare the skill, trade, service, or product that a man can provide. This foundational understanding is timeless and undeniable. It doesn't matter what new fucking A.I. chat tool or computer-based system enters the world's marketplace; everyone will make money or not in relation to how they are based on those factors. You can make excuses or make money, but you can't make both. Generating less money than the lifestyle you have chosen is called Poverty. That really sucks.

Poverty creates a suffocating amount of stress that can often give the illusion there is no way out. Poverty leads to agony. having to decide between buying enough food for your children and paying the rent is a fork in the road that makes you wanna head back the other way. When the struggle of financial hardship settles into a man's way of being, it begins to affect his beliefs, optimism, and entire outlook on life. Not being able to order a pizza or go eat out with friends for a weekend or two is not what I am talking about here. There's a huge difference between being strapped for cash and feeling destitute. It's the feelings associated with the perception of the situation that can steal a man's joy, making him feel hopeless.

You may not be able to change the number on that bank statement at this moment, but you can instantly change what you think it says about WHO YOU ARE. And who I say you are, is a mother fucking KING!

Let me be clear; income and resources are significant, but they are not the only things that are important. A high-income-earning asshole that thinks he is better than everyone else because of his money, just makes him broke on another level. Some people are so broke that all they have is money. FACTS.

Money can buy you a clock.
But Money can't buy you time.

Money can buy you a house.
But Money can't buy you a home.

Money can buy you a bed.
But Money can't buy sleep.

Money can buy a doctor's visit.
But Money can't buy Good Health.

While being broke sucks and being financially rich isn't everything, the satisfaction of your ability to produce income has a major effect on your happiness. FACTS. You must understand how important it is to control your perception, which affects your feelings about your money, before it changes. There's a reason why successful brands have profited off of making people feel good for spending more money than they should. It makes them feel good to impress others with status symbols, even when important expenses are being neglected. Whoever popularized the phrase *"Fake it till you make it"* has killed way more entrepreneurs than

Income

the recession. FACTS. This bullshit advice planted a giant weed of wastefulness in my garden that strangled the fuck out of my income flowers for years. Someone cast this cliche like a spell on me so that I would blow most of my money on things I really didn't want, to impress people that didn't matter, so they would think I was doing better than I really was. What a fucking charade. If I could go back in time and change this for every other person infected by it, simply replacing one word in that statement: *"You gotta **FACE IT, till you MAKE IT!**"* Being honest with yourself about the decisions you have made regarding money won't be easy. It was not easy for me. But the best time to start doing the right thing was yesterday, and the second-best time is today!

I thought I wanted a Lamborghini until I actually sat inside one. My good friend Kevin invited me for an opportunity to drive one on a racetrack in Las Vegas, and I didn't like being inside of it at all. From the outside, it was sexy and sleek, with all its music video aura and appeal. But with spaceship-like buttons everywhere, practically sitting on the ground, and damn, it was loud – It made me realize this wasn't my style. Wanting that car was not **MY** true heart's desire. I wanted the association of what I thought successful men should drive. WRONG. Copying someone else's dream can easily become your nightmare. Determine what serves you, as opposed to what impresses others. Spin the dial on what you spend money on every month, if you're landing on impressing others and getting instant gratification, you know it will cost you more. By the way, it costs more money to be broke. If I added up just the money in bank overdrafts and late penalty fees, I could've saved myself from bankruptcy. The habits in my life were not congruent with keeping money. My mom used to say, "Lerrod, keeping up with the Joneses will make you a day late and a dollar short."

My manner of dealing with income wasn't just a problem I needed to deal with as an individual. My behavior had real consequences for the rest of my family. My lasciviousness had an impact on the people that I claimed I was doing all this hard work for. Only when the repercussions of my choices began to affect my kids could I see it clearly enough to make a change. The concept of income is not just about having money. It is also the way in which you generate it, grow it, and protect it. How many sources of income do you require to live the life that you desire? Do you want to make money more passively to pursue non-income-bearing pursuits? These are the things you must consider when you look at how you want to make your income. It starts when we are children. Most kids get forced onto a train called "What you wanna do when you grow up?" This train, more often than not, stops at stations like, "This place fucking Sucks." And "I never wanted to do this lane," And finally, when years go by, the last stop is "Regretville" after realizing you wasted your whole life chasing money through jobs that weren't paying enough or fulfilling anyway. ALL ABOARD!

SCARCITY

When you're behind on your bills and experience a lack of resources, you will only focus on survival. This is the breeding ground for the most poisonous creature in the world, Scarcity. This is like a snake that will strangle your ability to think clearly, and the fear will inject a venom of selfishness into your life, causing you to destroy relationships and compromise your values. Scarcity is contagious and insidious because you don't realize that it is your fear as the problem perpetuates more problems. We think it's the lack of money that we have right now that is our problem. However, it is our habits and decisions that have placed us in these situations. Therefore, being scared of not having cash causes you to think more about suffering, instead of changing the poor character that got you there!

You think making a ton of money will solve all of your problems? NOT. If you had more money, you would just create more problems, because more money only makes you more of what you already are. If you are a giver and a wonderful person, you will become a generous philanthropist and build charitable organizations. If you are wasteful and selfish, you will become eccentric, lonely, and a collector of things. Does that sound like what you want? No.

BE, DO, HAVE

Most of us are taught by society that we must first have something so that we can do something, and then we become something. For example, Imagine the train of thought that starting a business requires lots of money. Then, if you could somehow get a large sum of money, you can launch and run a successful business. Ultimately, by building an income producing business you will by default become successful and wealthy. This is absolutely false. Some of the greatest entrepreneurial success stories in the world started with a few dollars, required hard work, and had a clear dream. But what comes first, the cart or the horse? Instinctively you might think it's the horse because it's out front pulling the cart, however if you consider that if there was no cart to pull there would be no need for the damn horse. The Dream must always come first. You as the dreamer must first be capable of having it before you require the resources to make it happen. SUPER FACTS.

You must first BE it, then DO it so that you can HAVE it.

This principle can be applied to every area of your life as well. A dog does not need to be taught to bark; the same way a cat doesn't need to be taught to climb a tree. it's natural to the fabric of it's being. When the person who you are BEING, is congruent with the goals that you HAVE, then you will DO what is required to get your S.H.I.T. together. This could be your next tattoo.

You don't get out of life what you want.

You get out of life who you are.

- Eric Thomas

I was operating backward, thinking if I had the RIGHT amount of money, I would do the RIGHT thing, then I would become the RIGHT wealthy person. That should make sense, RIGHT? However, the root of my failure was not my lack of ability to earn money. Rather, it was spending like an asshole that was breaking me. I didn't do the things that made me worthy of wealth and abundance. Therefore, no matter how much money I would make or save up, it would be gone quickly, leaving me worse off than before.

An important element of managing income is not overspending. So how do you do it? The most successful at the money game use principles and systems to control the flow of their income. Some people use budgets to help them operate from a place of scarcity. Those who are untrained in the art of money are always on the hunt for a new way to budget their finances into order. By the way, that was how the old me did it.

During one of my low points, I shared a notebook full of my get-rich plans with a good friend and mentor, Coach Kevin, where he said this profound statement, *"Lerrod, you can't budget your way to wealth!"* -DEEP! Budgets are great tools, and they have their place for stopping cash leaks and curbing your nonsense spending. However, you first need to create enough income to produce abundance. From there, you can move toward wealth. It's impossible to budget *not enough* income into prosperity. I am not suggesting anyone ignore the value of having a solid budget for their money. Just make sure your focus is on making enough money first. Worrying about paying your bills each month can put you into the miserable mentality of brokenness!

If you are struggling and need a simple formula, do this:

- Open three separate bank accounts, one for incoming deposits, the second for personal expenses, and the third for saving.
- Set up automatic bill pay for all of your fixed living expenses like rent, electricity, and phone bills to pay out from account number one.

Income

- Set automatic transfer of a consistent, un-changing amount into account two as money for personal use. Such as groceries, entertainment, transportation, etc.
- Set up an automatic monthly transfer of 10% of your income into your savings account that you don't touch.

Thinking about paying your bills every day leads you to BEING stressed, which leads to bad decisions, which leads to BEING broke. Now broke is bad. However, there are things far worse.

People interchangeably use the words "broke" and "poor" all of the time as if they mean the same thing. But there's a huge difference between being broke and being poor. The first is measured at the bank, and the second is recognized in the mind. It's not as simple as the amount of money you have access to. Broke is about what you HAVE now, whereas POOR is about WHO you are BEING. To be broke means to not have enough money for what you want or require. That's all it means. Nothing else. Someone who's "broke" might not have enough money to cover a bill or go on a vacation right now, but tomorrow is another day. In the game of money that status could change in an instant with one strong move on the board.

Being Poor is a contagious mindset that spreads and infects people like a contagious virus. It's like a pandemic, but the only people with masks on are the wealthy. POOR is so insidious because people share their fears and beliefs with everybody they know. Some of us even believe we are doing GOD's work by helping you to be meek, safe, and cautious. However, they are really just expressing their worry and doubts about being in abundance. My favorite scientific principle is in physics, which states, "two separate things cannot occupy the same space at the same time." So that means thinking like your poor and thinking like your rich can't happen together; one of those fuckers has gotta go. Not actually making money requires a much longer discussion than we're going to have here. I'm going to focus on Income and its relation to your mindset and control for getting your **S.H.I.T** together. If you want to be financially healthy, stop looking at the current state of your pockets, and change, WHO you are FINACIALLY BEING.

I have learned a few valuable lessons from some very rich people. The power of money goes beyond just the numbers in your bank account, you gotta talk like you are ready to make money, Otherwise you're gonna end up broke. It's not just your words but your actions that will have you communicating in what I call POOR man's language. Every language is derived from a place, by a set of people, based on their environment. Whales live in the ocean, gorillas live in the forest, and hawks live in the sky, and they all communicate with each other in languages that match their conditions. Often, people who are raised in poverty or, by circumstance, end up in poverty learn to speak this wicked dialect. The language is riddled with adjectives of fear, verbs of doubt, and most of the nouns relate to things which are believed out of reach or attainability. An important thing to know about this is most people who are using this language have no idea that they are using it. And if you're speaking POOR, Man, what do you think that the people around you are hearing from you? Also, you should listen closely, with a fresh ear, to the conversation of the people that you hang around most. When we cannot see the bullshit in ourselves directly, we can scrutinize our friend group, because we are just reflections of the people, we spend the most time with. Statistics say we only make within a few thousand dollars difference of the five people we speak to most. We must choose to speak differently and possibly choose different people to speak to. When we begin to communicate differently, we act differently, and people will respect us differently.

Most of us were raised by people who don't speak the language of money, so it stands to reason that they could not have taught it to us. Salute to Robert Kiyosaki's book 'Rich Dad, Poor Dad.' As a kid, I was indoctrinated with the idea that money was hard to make, doesn't grow on trees, and our last name definitely wasn't Rockefeller. I bet you know someone who was raised with that poor-man conversation, too. When I got into the entrepreneurial world, I brought that poor man chatter with me, which was terrible. Without me realizing it, most of the highly successful, positive-minded entrepreneurs I came in contact with couldn't understand my pessimistic, anti-rich guy language. If you want to make real money, you must be able to network with get-money-people and learn their language. You can actually speak rich by just understanding and operating in a certain way around money. This book is not about how to make more money, but the objective is to help you believe and understand that it's possible for you to have it. There are thousands of books on strategies for making and investing money, and in the G.M.S.T. community we share the best resources that we find with each other for getting things done.

'WE' means that you don't have to do it alone. By surrounding yourself with other men, taking the Get My S.H.I.T Together (G.M.S.T.) challenge will give you energy and positive conversation about income. Over time, your commitment and dedication, surrounded by other kings who share these ideas, will fortify you into a brand-new man worthy of the king's riches.

The Bottom Line

Where attention goes, energy flows, so whatever you think about, you bring about. I first learned these concepts from Rhonda Burn's book The Secret, which preaches the metaphysical Law of Attraction. Regardless of your beliefs about this, no one can deny the truth that focusing more on what you want gets you closer to what you want. Therefore, on the other side, if you spend a lot of time thinking and speaking about all of your money problems, that just brings you more money problems.

Trying to live someone else's dream is a one-way ticket to your own personal nightmare. I was caught up in the whirlwind of trying to impress others with my spending habits. But believe me when I say this - it costs you so much more to be broke than you might think. The slap of reality hit me hard when I saw the impact of my actions on my kids, and I knew I had to make a change.

The thing is, income isn't just about the money in your bank account; it's about how you Make it, Grow it, and Protect it. Understand something crucial: when your backs against the wall financially, it's easy to fall into a scarcity mindset. But that mindset is like quicksand. it only drags you deeper into fear and "Poor Man" speaking and decision-making. The real issue isn't your current lack of money; it's the habits and decisions that got you to this point. Address the character issues that landed you here, and you'll find your way out.

Here's another hard truth: More money won't automatically fix your problems. In fact, it only magnifies who you already are. To truly be wealthy - in both mindset and material wealth - you have to shift your way of being. You've got to BE the person who deserves wealth, then DO the actions that lead to it, and you'll find yourself naturally HAVING it. I used to think that if I just made or saved more money, my problems would disappear. But the real shift came when I changed my habits and my mindset.

So, here's my final piece of advice: start with who you're being. Align your actions with your true self. Get your S.H.I.T. together by embodying the person you want to be, and the life you want will naturally follow. Trust me, I've been there, and I know it's possible. Just be committed and consistent.

"Champions do Daily what ordinary people do occasionally...

That doesn't make them Extraordinary, it just means they do the ordinary - Extra."

- Kenny Smith

ABUNDANCE vs. SCARCITY

There's a battle between abundance and scarcity. Abundance means to have much more than you require. When I have enough to share with others, and I have little concerns about continuing to have enough of this resource, then I am in abundance. That is wealth. Most men, as providers and leaders of households, want desperately to live in that space. Nobody wants to live with the concern of having less than what they require, struggling to maintain what they have, or always wanting something because they don't feel like they have enough.

Then there's scarcity. Scarcity is a mental space where "I don't have what I need, and I always feel that I don't have enough, even when I have what is required." Scarcity is very dangerous because it plagues your mind like fear. You could have more than enough resources to survive, to live, or do well, but you feel like you don't and worry that it's going to run out. You're worried that whatever you have is going to leave you, and you cannot share anything with others because you must get more for yourself. That was my life. Even when I sold property for big profits, even when I built businesses, even when I had more money than I needed to survive, I was suffering from the possibility that I didn't have enough, and I was going to lose what I had eventually. It was pure scarcity. Entrepreneurs living in scarcity are some of the most dangerous people in the world. Not only a danger to themselves, but to family and other people they influence. Entrepreneurs who are powerful leaders will drive followers into that same mindset of scarcity. They will build and create things because they're creators, and they will build and create things around scarcity.

We, as kings that are out to get big S.H.I.T. done, have to do it from the state of mind that we already have everything we need. Abundance is a state of mind. I could have no money in my pocket or bank account, but if I'm in a state of abundance, I will operate in a way that brings things to me. An abundance mindset can create and see opportunities that others in scarcity cannot and will not see.

Scarcity of time, money, relationships, or anything else does not serve you, King. You must eliminate the mindset that things will run out, or there won't be enough for you: that there is scarcity. There is no scarcity! There will always be enough for you to have more than you could want. This world provides it. Your mind has to be set in a focus that you are enough, you have enough, and you can create whatever you want. It is all up to you. There is a legitimate battleground that all real men will face every day, "Do I go forward and take ground, or do I retreat and protect what I have? Should I look to create more, or should I be worried about saving the little that I have?" You must choose which mindset serves you best as a KING.

If you are of this scarcity mindset and constantly thinking of what you lack, you will not have the power to focus on empowering the S.H.I.T. that matters to you. There is a war that's happening in your mind that's telling you to stop. And then there's a thing in your heart that's telling you, "I want to go." And I'm here to tell you, when I removed that bridge, and I destroyed it so that nothing in my mind, from that evil programming, could come down and contaminate my heart and drive to go forward, I just started to act! And before you knew it, I had built up enough things in my mind that showed me proof that I could do it and I could win.

Your mind is programmed based on what it sees. And if someone gives you faulty programming when you're a kid, they may have told you, "Hey, listen, based on all of these things that have happened, you will be poor. With all these things that happened, you will not have enough. Money is hard to get. People will hurt you. There are not enough relationships. You got to hurry up. You got to work twice as hard for half as much." And it will get you proof that your mind will use to now tell you that that's where you must be. You must live, king, from your imagination, not your memory, not based on the program that somebody else had. You must live in a mindset of creation. Imagination is creation.

I want it from my heart just because I want it, not because I saw it before, not because someone else had it. It's because I want it because I want it. That is abundance, and you can have it. It is yours. It's a battleground. It's a war between abundance and scarcity. It's happening right now. Where in your life are you? Are you living in abundance or scarcity?

Summary: Abundance vs. Scarcity

It's time to face the brutal truth: your life is a battlefield between abundance and scarcity. The stakes are high, and the consequences are real. If you're stuck in the scarcity mindset, you're poisoning your life, your relationships, and your dreams. It's time to destroy that toxic programming and embrace abundance with every fiber of your being.

Power Action Step:

- Awareness: Grab your journal and start by identifying the areas of your life where scarcity has been lurking. Examine your current beliefs about money and choose new beliefs that or congruent with someone deserving of success. Which you are!

- Rewrite your story: Replace the scarcity script with a new, empowering narrative of abundance. Challenge those old beliefs and replace them with affirmations that fuel your abundance mindset. Remember, it's not about what you've been through but where you're going.

- Take bold action: Armed with your new mindset, make decisions and take actions that reflect abundance. Whether it's investing in yourself, giving more to others, or taking calculated risks, show the world that you're not held back by scarcity anymore.

- Evaluate and adjust: Keep track of your progress in your journal. Reflect on your journey, celebrate your wins, and adjust as needed to stay on the path of abundance.

- The fight is on, and you're the commander of your destiny. Don't let scarcity dictate your life any longer. Embrace abundance and become the unstoppable force you were born to be.

CHAPTER FOUR
- TIME

The goal is to live a Life worth Living.

-Donald 'Cowboy' Cerone

If you are not happy and excited about life, then what's the fucking point? Just muddling through and surviving life is not living - you are just alive; there is a big difference. Plants are alive, insects are alive, and even bacteria are alive, but that doesn't mean they have a life called living. Have you ever thought about 'grass' living it's best life? Hell No. Time is the space between happiness and everything else. Have you noticed that when you are having the best experiences of your life, it's almost like the clock stopped, and you have some warped concept of how long you have been enjoying yourself? On the other hand, when you are in the middle of a life storm, it seems to be going on forever. We emotionally connect to time based on our internal happiness meter.

This is because time is really not what most people think it is. Time is distance. Time is only a measurement of the distance from one position to another. Land geography, space maps, and even the correlation of your house address on a real estate property deed are recognized by time. Without getting too granularly scientific about the subject, understand that the Earth spins around on an axis and has a positional relationship with the sun. Our entire time structure is based on the distance of where our physical position is or will be on Earth from the sun in rotation. For a super clear explanation of this, check out the video explainer on GetMyShitTogether.com. As for this conversation, let's consider what is happening in the distance of your life between doing what you love and the next thing that sucks.

"The average person Tiptoes through life,

Hoping to make it safely to their death.

- What a dumb game."

- Bob Proctor

I have plenty of things to occupy my time. There's an endless list of opportunities in business to consider opportunities to offer my attention to the wife and kids, opportunities to take care of myself, etc... Notice that I consider all of these functions as opportunities because I have a choice! I am a KING, meaning what I do with my time is fully in my control.

A pivotal point in my life was making the decision to invest my time in martial arts. I wanted something to challenge my body and my mind. I love to run long distances, but nothing gets my juices flowing like combat sports. I have always had an aggressive nature, so choosing MMA and Jiu Jitsu was an easy call.

No appointment, no call. I walked in off the street to Brooklyn Mixed Martial Arts and found exactly what I was looking for. The room looked like a UFC training center, filled with guys half my age rolling and sparring. No free intro class was required. I signed up on the spot. After one week of getting my ass kicked by almost everyone in the room, I signed up for a Jiu-Jitsu competition called NAGA Battle on the Beach as a challenge for my 42nd birthday. For the next 60 days, I trained twice a day, for six days a week. I would go for a run every morning and train at BKMMA in the evenings. I survived, thanks to Tiger Balm, Icy Hot, and a portable one-person sauna box stinking up the living room. It paid off big. Starting at 220 pounds, after 60 days, I successfully qualified for the 190 weight class at the tournament. Chiseled and proud, with my wife, kids, and friends all watching, I competed and won my division. This early tournament success set me on fire, so I went on a rampage, entering multiple Jiu-Jitsu tournaments month after month, racking up a wall full of medals. This proved to be a superior use of my time, as I have enjoyed every moment of developing myself into a healthy, fit, confident warrior.

From tournaments to super fights, I have experienced wins and losses, which have made me stronger and happier. At 46, I became an IBJJF Masters World Bronze medalist and No Gi World Champion. Since that's in the history books forever, I will always be proud of such a big accomplishment. Making it to the top of those podiums were my proof that time is under my control. I feel as if I just started Jiu Jitsu yesterday because the distance from when I started until now has been filled with happiness. But if instead of training and enjoying the sport that I love, I was chasing down extra money, doing a job I hated, that suffering would make it feel like the last few years was a damn eternity! Time is the distance between experience of happiness and not. FACTS.

A man who thinks he has **something** will do **NOTHING**.

A man who thinks he has **nothing** will do **ANYTHING**.

We should all behave like our **SOMETHING** could soon be **NOTHING**.

- King Smalls

Let's imagine yesterday you went to sleep knowing that you had zero dollars in your bank account. However, when you woke up this morning and checked your bank account, and it said you have $86,400! This can't be right! So you call the bank, and they verify that it was indeed deposited into your account by an unknown benevolent individual who will remain anonymous. There's a catch, though; a big one. The person who made the deposit left instructions requiring you to spend the entire amount today. If you don't, you lose everything left unspent. It is the biggest Use It or Lose it scenario you could imagine.

What would you do with that money? You could rush out and try to spend as much of it as you could on things that don't even matter just so you don't lose it. Or you could be conscious and only make select purchases for safe and practical things. Either way, when the lights go out, every last unused cent would be gone because you can't transfer it to the next day. You cannot bundle it up on top of the previous day. It doesn't build up. No rollover credit. Although by the grace of this incredible benefactor, tomorrow you would get another $86,400.

What if we were not talking about dollars and cents? What if we were talking minutes and Days? Twenty-four hours breaks down to 86,400 seconds using 3rd-grade math.

If you thought of your life in the same exact way, with No rollover minutes, you either use it or lose it! I am sure you would want to run that balance down to zero each and every day. I think of each day like the last supper, and I'm cleaning my plate and licking my fingers. My wish for you is - Don't leave a damn thing on the table. **I Want You to Live Full and Die Empty.**

I know it is easy to think we have an abundance of time, especially when you are young. I spent years flagrantly giving it away to people who did not deserve it. Many of us don't use our time for our own benefit, or we sell it too damn cheap at some job- am I right? If you knew how precious time was, you wouldn't sell it so cheap. Some people are busting their ass, working an hourly job for 40 hours a week for 40 years of their life and retiring on 40% of the income that wasn't enough in the first place! That 40/40/40 plan isn't spelled out quite like that in school, but you can bet that's the drug they are pushing.

Twenty years from now, you'll be wanting and wishing to be in the exact health, happiness, and state of being that you're in right now. Take a moment to consider how you feel about the possibility of going back 20 years ago and how grateful you would be for that opportunity and that youth. What would you be willing to give up for that option?

A life to be proud of is worth fighting for. If this were easy, every man would have their **S.H.I.T** together. A man with true happiness and respect is a man who sacrifices and who is willing to put in the real work internally and externally. Grinding hard on his finances to flourish for the benefit of his family and future. I suffered and struggled without getting the results I wanted until I became ruthlessly committed. Are you really willing to do what it takes? Every precious moment of your time is like currency to purchase a legendary life! Or you can squander minutes here and there, blowing time on nonsense, and whatever you have left settle for a mediocre existence.

How you answer that question and the sacrifices you make will determine what kind of life you will have.

If you decided to be accountable for your own life without the need to blame others or make excuses, then it's time to step into your role as a King. Be about that action. However, this is a choice you must make every day. Who do you want to be? Do you want to reign in a life that you designed or be ruled by the circumstances you have created?

Anything that is alive requires growth. Nothing is exempt from this principle. Change must be constant and deliberate for something to continue living. Things get old, deteriorate, and die because they stop growing. Ideas, beliefs, and businesses all start dying the moment they become stagnant. Here is a scenario I want you to consider... Everyone has a favorite chair or piece of furniture they appreciate most in the house. For this example, imagine it's a chair. You take that chair outside and put in the back yard of your house and leave it. In this story, nobody steals it, moves it, or even touches the chair. It just remains uncovered and exposed in the same spot.

Now, as life goes on, your chair has been sitting outside for two years, then three years, then five years. Only allowed to stay in that one place. When you finally go out to examine the chair, what do you expect to see? Do you believe it will be in better condition, The same condition, or in worse condition than when you left it in that spot? Now, I've asked this question to thousands of people all around the country, and overwhelmingly, everyone says that it would be in worse condition. They give answers like because of the rain, the sun beating on it, and the wear and tear of stormy weather. All of these things are elements that affect the chair while it's sitting still and doing nothing. The chair, over time, became less than, beaten up, uglier, and weaker.

But now I would have you consider, what if we replace the word chair with your name? What if the story was about a man that is YOU? The guy that graduates school gets a job, starts a family, then, slowly dies for 40 years in a cubicle of a job he hates. Or maybe he stays still in a dysfunctional marriage, numb from drinking and cheating on repeat. Or maybe stuck in place inside of a fat meat sack of a body, taking every day to stay alive. What if you were doing nothing of substance and your life was a boring circle day after day, year after year? How do you think you would look? Here is why the problem is so insidious: we put lipstick on the pig and make it look like life is pretty as can be. Social media might have some great before and after photos of the story of how your life is going, but the truth is on the inside. Only YOU KNOW if you are rotting because you have not been growing, and only you can do something about it.

Do you get it? Losing is the default we get when we stop growing and developing. <u>Reminder</u> - One of the greatest lessons anyone can learn in this life is "When we **stop fighting** for what we DO want, we **automatically** get what we DON'T want!

I've been there. At my lowest financial point, just before I declared bankruptcy, I was eating garbage and looking like a complete mess. I was unhealthy and soft. Drinking and socializing every day to escape in my mind what my situation enslaved me to. When I dedicated myself to personal development, I realized I wasn't alone. I was amongst a tribe of men feeling the same way. We were losing! We definitely have our heroes and champions who have excelled and set an example for us. However, when you look from a 10,000-foot view at the statistics of issues that matter, like income, education, divorce, health, political influence, and generational wealth, as a collective, we are at the bottom.

The elements, the world, and our everyday life are constantly attacking us, beating us down. If we do not move, the elements win. Not only will we not grow, but eventually, we end up dying inside. Tuff.

Every Minute Matters

The only thing God gave us when we came into this world was time. You didn't come into this place with cars, clothes, jewelry, women, or anything else that you see, or you may idolize right now. No one did. No one was better than you. God sent you into this world, kicking and screaming, butt-ass naked, with time and the ability to make decisions, and because you have that, you have to treasure it, value it. It is the most important, critical thing you have in your world.

If you want to get S.H.I.T. done, you have to measure and manage the only thing that allows you to get S.H.I.T. done. That's time. Every year, there are 365 days. And of those 365 days, you have 24-hour segments that are broken up into minutes. I call it the 1440 because there are 1440 minutes in every single day. Each one of them matters. I think people have started to discredit and devalue what a minute is, what it is all about. What can I do with it? Why should I measure it? Why should I manage it? Why should I even consider it? It's only a minute. It's 60 seconds. I can be there. I can do that in a minute. I can give you a minute.

If every time someone asks you to give them a minute, they had to actually give you some money; people would stop asking for your time. Because we give it away so freely, people ask for it, and they even demand it from us for nothing. People will waste it by just interjecting and stopping you from doing the S.H.I.T. that matters to you. You will give it away frivolously to things like Instagram, Facebook, LinkedIn, and Twitter. But not because you're doing business, just because you're scrolling and paying attention to somebody else's S.H.I.T.

Each minute matters. Minutes are like money, because time is the currency of life. My mom said this to me years ago, " Watch the pennies, and the dollars will take care of themselves." By making sure that from minute to minute you are being productive and enjoying those minutes you're guaranteed to have a good hour. And if you have a collection of good hours, then you'll have a good day. If you have a collection of good days, then it'll be a good week, which turns into a good month. And with 2nd grade pattern recognition you can see how good years will be created, by having successful years, you ultimately have a successful life. POW!

Can you see how simple it is to control the quality of time in your life? You don't have to see the entire plan for your life, or know all of the right decisions to be made to be a huge success. Those are way too big for us to see anyways. Those things are important, and you should go after them. We will go after them. But what you have to deal with right now is your minutes; that's 1,440 of them every single day. From the moment that your eyes open and your feet hit the ground, you are in charge of 1440 minutes. How are you

---

going to treat every single one of them? Do you know how you're going to use them, how you're going to invest them, how you're going to spend them, or if you're going to allow someone to steal them or if you're going to give them away?

I believe in charity. I believe in investing. I believe that giving to others is a blessing. And yes, I donate my time, I give my time, I invest my time, and I share my time, but not until I do S.H.I.T. for me first. I wake up in the morning, and I give most of my time to myself first. 10% of my day, two-and-a-half hours, is dedicated to me every morning before I talk to anybody else. Fuck everybody else. It's my time. That's the most important thing. I protect my minutes first. Then everybody else can get what comes after that.

I can't give you what I don't have. If I don't have peace of mind, I can't give you that. If I don't have a strong body and health, I can't help you. If I don't have a family and love, I can't share love with you. If I haven't dedicated time to my business, I can't give you money or support myself. And, if I haven't spent time planning for my future, I ultimately will crumble, and the generations behind me will die and will never grow to be their full potential.

Can you see how 1440 is so critical, so important? Your 1440 is the most important and powerful thing that you can imagine. Time is your friend only if you don't give it away or let it be stolen by other people. This is for you. This message can change your life forever. It should have changed your life forever. It has changed mine. My family's life will never be the same because I get to invest in my children the thoughts and ideas that I've shared with you in this program.

Now, it's time for you to get your S.H.I.T. together. No more talking about it. No more thinking about it. You don't have to ask me permission, and you don't need permission from anybody else. Don't send me an email asking more questions. Just do what I've laid out in this program. Attack what matters to you most. Again, it's time to get <u>YOUR</u> S.H.I.T. together.

Nuff said.

The Bottom Line

Time is the most precious resource in this world. FACTS.

Time is ticking by, and it's the one thing you can't negotiate with, bribe, or win back. Every second that slips through your fingers is a moment of your life that you'll never experience again. There is no rewinding, no turning back the hands of the clock. So, ask yourself, why are you wasting it? That's rhetorical because I know that if you realized it, you would not. We think we always have a little more time than we actually do. Every second matters and counts, and we have to consider that with every decision to do or not do something.

Time

When I practice Jiu Jitsu, it is not just about strangling people or breaking limbs, it is about learning and understanding life in its most primal, unfiltered form. Life is a relentless, unforgiving fight, and if you're not all in, you're getting choked out. If it feels like life has taken you by the back and is beating your head in. You are not special or unique. Hundreds of generations of men that have come before you have experienced worse. But not wasting time crying about it and being willing to face it head on is the ideal reaction. Now, take this as a challenge, grab it with both hands, and tackle it head-on. Engage with it. Fight it with everything you've got. Push yourself to the very edge of your limits because that's how you achieve an extraordinary life.

There was a time when I sold my time cheaply. Scratch that. I practically gave it away for free. But now? Now, I recognize my worth. I treasure every single second of my existence like it's a nugget of pure gold. And you should, too. Don't squander it on trivialities and nonsense. Live large. Live boldly. Aim for the stars. Aim for the stuff of legends.

Feeling like your time has passed and you are too late? I've been there too. Believe me, as a middle-aged black man in America, with a life expectancy of 72, I know that feeling well. But here's the hard truth: you're not a tree rooted to one spot; you have the power to move, to change, to break free, and go do whatever the fuck you want to do now! So, no more excuses, no more waiting for 'someday' or 'tomorrow.'

This is it. Your one chance at life. Don't wait around for life to happen to you. Take the chances and MAKE IT HAPPEN.

Remember that chair outside, beaten down and eroded by time and the elements? That's you if you choose to sit around idly, waiting for something to change. If you're content with mediocrity, by all means, stay seated. But if you hunger for excellence, if you want to taste greatness, then stand up. Rise to your feet. Challenge yourself. Push yourself beyond what you thought was possible. There's a king or queen inside of you, waiting to be acknowledged, waiting to be crowned. It's about damn time you did the honors. The Marines use a Latin saying "Carpe Diem," which means Seize the Day. I say, "OWN THAT MOTHER FUCKER."

Lastly, you came into this world with nothing but time, and that's your greatest asset! Everything else – the cars, the clothes, the jewels – it's all just background noise. You were born kicking and screaming, with the clock already ticking, and it hasn't stopped since.

Time is your currency! There are 1440 minutes in a day, no more, no less. Stop treating your minutes like they're worthless. Every time you say, "I'll give you a minute," you're handing over your most valuable resource. Stop letting people rob you of your time with their distractions, their demands, their nonsense.

You think scrolling through social media is harmless? You're spending your minutes on other people's S.H.I.T., not your own! Each minute you waste is a minute you can't get back.

My mom used to say, "Watch the pennies, and the dollars will take care of themselves." Well, watch your minutes, and the hours, days, and years will fall into place. You don't need to have your whole life mapped out; just start with today, with this moment.

1440 minutes – that's what you've got every day. What are you going to do with them? Are you going to invest them in yourself, spend them wisely, or let others take them from you?

I give my time to others that are worthy, but I take the first 10%, 144 minutes, for my damn self. You can't pour out anything from an empty cup, so take care of your minutes, and you will have enough personal value to share lessons and blessings with others.

Time's ticking. Make it count. Stop wasting it on things that don't matter. Focus on your own S.H.I.T., and you'll build a life that's worth living.

FOCUS vs. SCATTER

There's a war going on for you to be either focused or scattered.

Looking at the sun, the sun is beaming down, with lots of light, powerful heat, and radiating light on the planet, warming up the whole place, which is good for us, healthy for the Earth. Man, if you were to take even a fraction of that sunlight and channel it through the correct tool and vehicle, which could be a laser, it can channel all of it and focus it into one small, small spot, which will create a very powerful and focused laser beam. Now the light is the same, but it's scattered all around. When you collect it, and focus it and channel it, it becomes more powerful.

So, what does that analogy mean for you? You're probably thinking "I gotta get focused." F.O.C.U.S. The great acronym, Follow One Course Until Successful. That's correct. I've been saying it for years, and it's absolutely true. But see, what we must do when we're getting our S.H.I.T. together, is to separate it in the battle. See, there's a battle that we have to be prepared for. The battle is the scatter. The battle is that we have all these different things that are taking away time from our focus. We are focusing on something. We have to pay attention to it, but we will **actively choose**, to promote and do multiple things at the same time.

So, we set up legitimate, real targets! These are not things that we just consider as distractions. No, no, no, no. These are not nonsense things. These are things that have real results at the end of it that we desperately want. We want these things, right? For example, say, I want to own some property, and I also want to own cryptocurrency, and I also want to own a construction, and I also want to own a restaurant. This list is never ending, and these are all good things. In fact, these are great things. However, you cannot get them all done at the same time. You can do anything, but you cannot do everything. You cannot scatter the force that you have. You must channel it around one thing and produce one worthy result. That's for you. Nobody else can determine what that that one particular thing is.

When it comes to your finances, are you doing multiple different businesses at the same time, where you can't even get enough energy and focus to make sure you got that one thing done that could fund the other things. One of the men who built America, Andrew Carnegie said, "many men try to have eggs in each of their baskets, so that their eggs aren't in one basket, but those men never become very successful. The men that become very successful put all of their eggs into one basket, and they watch like hell over that basket."

So first, I'm gonna ask you what areas of your life are getting most of your attention? Then ask yourself, which area will have the most powerful impact on my life and improving my S.H.I.T.? Then lastly, Can I focus and put all of my energy into one particular thing and get that done with no distractions? That's how you create the real power. What are you willing to make a contract with yourself about and commit to eliminate the scatter of distraction from other things? See, these things are disguised to look very good and productive, but they will take you away from the most valuable one that you choose. Hopefully it's for rebuilding your S.H.I.T.

Now, for the battleground.

Summary: Focus vs. Scatter

In a world where attention is scarce, focus is your most powerful weapon. But focus isn't just handed to you; it's earned through discipline and practice. Stop scattering your energy and resources, and channel your focus to achieve greatness.

Power Action Step:

- Determine your top priorities: Clearly identify the most important areas of your life that demand your focus. Narrow it down to a few key aspects.
- Create a plan of attack: Develop a strategic plan outlining the specific steps and actions needed to achieve your goals in each priority area.
- Commit to a daily focus routine: Dedicate time each day to deep, focused work on your priorities. Establish a routine that promotes mental clarity and eliminates distractions.

- Regularly review and adjust: Assess your progress and adjust your approach as needed. Continually refine your focus to ensure you're always moving forward with   purpose.

CHAPTER FIVE
- THE WRAP UP

We've arrived at the point where you should understand the point by now. Hopefully, you know exactly what it means to get your S.H.I.T. together. You're probably saying, "I'm bout to get my shit together!" Since you made it this far, now it's time to wrap a bow on this conversation. The great John C. Maxwell has a training called the 'Four Seasons' in which people actually do something about their situation.

He said people change:

- When they hurt enough, they have to.
- When they have seen enough, they are inspired to.
- When they learn enough, they want to.
- When they receive enough, they are able to.

This is a real S.H.I.T. changer!

Whenever someone tells me that they are finally ready to stop the bullshit and get a new life, I ask myself, what season are they in? Are they just blowing smoke up my ass, or are they really in a season of change?

... Now it's your turn to ask yourself this same question. Before you can go even one step further, you should know without a shadow of a doubt if you are inside one or more of these seasons. Yes, you could be in the perfect storm, experiencing them all at the same time. If the answer is yes for even one of these seasons, buckle up and give yourself the green light to keep going because shit is about to get real, fast. Now, all there is left to do is to learn a formula of actions that you can do once you have made the commitment to change in the right season of change.

The Formula

What you do unconsciously, predictably, and regularly determines the long-term results you get for anything. YOU ARE YOUR HABITS AND ROUTINES. Therefore, if you want to change anything about yourself for good, you MUST change the things you do every day. And if you want your whole life to change, prepare to change almost everything you do in this way. You could absolutely accelerate your understanding of this by reading Atomic Habits by James Clear, where he breaks down the diabolical way our smallest of habits have a gigantic impact on our lives. I highly recommend this book!

So, how do you do this? What's the formula? What's the strategy? The first thing to know is you will never be finished getting your S.H.I.T together... Never. This is an always and forever thing. Understand me clearly: you will never get it completely right and be done with this process. You and I both will be on this journey until the fat lady sings. What I am offering you is a system of repeatable actions that can become routines, that get you what you want. Ultimately, when these daily routines become habits, you will unconsciously build a life of incredible results. And just like building any kind of structure, from a castle made of Legos to a skyscraper in a city, everything starts with a foundation.

Building a strong foundation in life is crucial, because everything else rests upon it. These are the "Foundational Five" pillars which support a complete life:

- **Faith** - Connecting and honoring a higher power or purpose than yourself.
- **Family** – Providing and nurturing joy and support with your spouse, children, and loved ones.
- **Fitness** - Taking care of your physical health through exercise and nutrition.
- **Finance** - Developing skills and systems to generate income abundantly and efficiently.
- **Fun** - Incorporating enjoyment and love into the above foundational areas.

<u>Faith</u> is tapping into purpose through belief - not just following some religion. Faith gives you fuel and guidance.

Having faith isn't being blindly optimistic, it's connecting with a higher source of strength and meaning. <u>Faith</u> is your spiritual connection to what you believe powers your world. Being aligned in faith helps you to handle challenges, knowing that they will always come. <u>Family</u> provides joy, support, and reminders of what matters most. Relationships recharge you and build closeness. Accepting help requires vulnerability but strengthens bonds. Physical and mental health are linked. <u>Fitness</u> is caring for your body and lifting up your mind, too. Small, consistent actions make big improvements over time. Being physically fit and having good nutrition gives you energy and affects your state of being. Money allows the exchange of value and the pursuit of your goals. <u>Finance</u> is about developing all of the required skills required to support you and your dreams. True wealth is the opportunities money can create, not just the amount of money that you have. Joy and fascination renew your spirit and spark creativity. <u>Fun</u>, laughter, and playing are what make life worth living. Connecting fun with everything that you do provides balance in your life and encourages you to do more of the things that require a strong foundation. Making time for fun reconnects you with gratitude, which is the pinnacle of all happiness. These foundational areas should seem interconnected with the controls of your S.H.I.T. – To remove any confusion, you might be having with the concepts of Foundation and S.H.I.T, consider this:

The Wrap Up

Faith, Family, Fitness, Finance, and Fun are about

What you are ***DOING***.

Story, Health, Income, and Time are about

Who you are ***BEING***.

Now it's time for action. Doing what is required is just as important as becoming qualified to have it. And going forward, it's going to start with getting up early. Every single day, you have to be the one that gets up before everybody else. There's a system for this. It means that the early bird gets the worm. It means the first people who get up and get active in the day have more opportunities to take action in the day because they use more of the day. Everybody's got 24 hours a day. A certain number of seconds, a certain amount of minutes, turn a certain amount of hours into a complete fucking day. So how is it that some people get more out of the day? How is it that some people actually produce great S.H.I.T. with their lives? These champions are on rocket ships getting real results; meanwhile, others seem to just be on rollercoasters struggling for peace of mind.

I can tell you that most of the high achievers I know, which I have been blessed to know many, all wake up before the sun does. They're up in the morning before sunrise, usually first in their house to get moving. They're already preparing themselves for the day. Everything must be built, including a life worth living. Therefore, I am going to introduce you to the concept of building FOUNDATION. From my experience in construction, buying, and repairing houses, the first thing that must be developed is a strong level foundation. The size of any structure is completely dependent on the design and strength of the base that it sits on, from a single-level ranch house to a cloud-touching skyscraper. So, let's walk through step-by-step exactly how you build a powerful foundation for some big ass results you can create every day. The following is a proven routine, tested through years of commitment by scores of men who have work tirelessly to get their S.H.I.T. together. However, anyone can modify the details, timing, and order as long as it's done as your first act of the day and has the five key elements. With consistency, your day has no other option but to submit to your will as you run the day. every day belongs to you. You own it. Carpe diem!

Grand Rise. When I first get up in the morning, there is no rush, no cell phone checking, or major discussions with anyone. I thank God, I thank the universe, and I thank myself because I'm grateful that I finally got up, knowing that I could have been one of those people who didn't wake up. See, gratitude opens the door to blessings. When you're grateful for things, and you have that spirit, receiving is the very next thing that happens. My first movement of the morning is to let out the waste from the night; sometimes a number one, or number two, or both. Relieving yourself naturally, lets your body react to your decisions around food and creates a fresh start in a physical way. This process is immediately followed by replacing the moisture that I need to create new cells and flush away the waste I will create. That's the process. Let it out, then let it in.

Drink water. Plain. Uncontaminated. Water. Your body is dehydrated. You need water to run all the functions of your body, including the most important, which is your brain. Many people will go through an entire day without having pure H2O. I prefer high-alkaline water because it has been proven to improve resistance to disease and responsiveness. If you don't have that, take a glass of water with a slice of lemon to slightly alkalize the water. Making this your first consumption of the day, you are telling your body you are turned on and prepared for action. This is a simple step, but it is absolutely critical. Your body is mostly water and requires water. And if you want the rest of the steps to work, you need to give your body exactly what it needs in order to lubricate your mind and your thoughts and get out of a space of dehydration.

Now, the very next thing I do is get myself into a place where I can meditate. I use a variety of different tools. Log on to GetMyShitTogether.com to find links for guided meditations and other tools we have available. Now, as you advance, you may not want guided meditations, and you'll be able to just quiet and still your mind and give yourself a clearing and a space. Why do you do that? Because it's easier to work in a clean environment. Have you ever worked at your desk? And it's full of clutter and junk. It just seems like you can't get your mind together and things just are not working out? Or you're in your bedroom and don't want to be there because there are clothes and mess all over the place? Or maybe that's just me.

But if that's you too, then it's the same thing that's happened in your mind. If you've got random thoughts all over the place of nonsense, things you must do, or even things you should have done. These things may be seriously fucking you up right now, but you have to calm your mind and get rid of it. You have to clear your space, clear the desk of your brain, if you will, so that you will now have a clean operating space to have fresh new thoughts that you put there that weren't put there by other people or dropped into the world from media or anything else. Now, as a side note, do not engage in social media. That is the biggest distraction and the worst thing you could do when your mind has been first waking up in the morning.

Your mind is an empty space, and now you get to choose what to fill it with. If you open up news, social media, radio, or any other form of contaminant, you're now being supported by that particular resource. Do not do it. It's hard. I know. I'm a victim of it myself, but you have to set yourself up for success. And that means turning off all alerts from all communication. No calls, emails, Facebook, Twitter, texting, or anything else that rings-dings or bings. Do not receive or engage with any of those tools when you are in the foundational stage of your morning. They will be there when you are done, but this time is for you. You are the captain of the ship, and you would not allow another captain to come in and subdue your organization or redirect your ship, would you? Most importantly, do not let the BAD NEWS media outlets influence you with their negativity bullshit. In the morning, our minds are the most vulnerable and accepting of ideas, and if you allow agenda-based news sources to contaminate your thoughts with every terrible thing that is happening around the world, that's exactly how you will feel. Terrible. This time is only for you.

Now, after a powerful meditation, you need to get your thoughts out. This is when it is time to take out the journal. Journal entries are absolutely powerful. It gives you the ability to write down what it is that you feel and what it is that you think coming out of meditation. Sometimes its gobbledygook, and sometimes, it's nothing. But sometimes, it's powerful. Sometimes it is scripture. What more are the thoughts of the Bible? The word of God, thoughts of men, stories, whatever you want to say. These are powerful ideas, strategies, or things that have come to somebody, and they wrote them down. So, what makes you any different? Why could you not build your own book? The book of you. Every day I am creating the book of Lerrod, it's full of my life and some powerful scriptures I have learned. It's my journal. I have a box full of them. No one needs a Hemingway-looking leather-bound thing with metal buckles on the side of it. Although that would be cool as fuck. It just needs to be honest. I will leave mine to my children so that they can pick it up and know exactly what was in my heart and the best of what I learned during my time here. These journals become priceless, especially in the later years, and even more so to the next generation. Journaling is an important part of building your foundation.

Next, I am going to share my love with those that matter most. By pouring encouragement and gratitude into my family, I'm reminding them of what they mean to me and setting them up for success for their day. Showing love and acknowledgment to my family for even the smallest of things and letting them know that I care matters, because they are now ready to support and love me back. Sometimes I send text messages to my children or leave them a note in their room. I'm writing a journal entry of love to my wife and share it with her. I'm sending gratitude messages to old friends. I'm issuing a signal out to the people in my world saying I care about you. Doing all of these gestures does not insulate me from conflict or disagreements, but it sets the stage for a great start in the day's conversation with people that matter.

Don't overlook this. Sending these messages out to people who you care about is important. And even beyond your family, send those out to your business partners; send those out to people you know. Randomly send it to people who you've had experiences with. You will be surprised by how you could change someone's entire life by just showing them that you care about them. There are too many documented instances that a well-timed gratitude note could keep a brother who is on the edge of suicide from putting that bullet in their head. Maybe that seems extreme for those in your network, but guess what? Do it! Because you never know what is happening in the shadow of your people's lives. That's important. Sending gratitude is just as important as eating food because it fuels and energizes the people around you, who will, in turn, energize and love you.

Now, after I've shown love to everyone else in the world, it's time to respect this machine. It's time to do something for myself. That puts me in power. So, I'm off to the gym. I'm either leaving the house to the gym, or I'm going down and working out in my house, or I'm running in the street. Whatever it is, you have to do to build up a sweat. It's time to activate your body. Your body has endorphins that have to be activated. Your body has things that have to be moved. You have to show your body that you're in charge and you're willing to work it. And if you don't, you'll lose it. The saying goes anything you don't use, you will lose. So, if you don't move it, you will lose it. So, get out there and do something. Put your body in a state of pressure. Force it to sweat. Push it to a limit. Do something that will get your body in a position to know that you are using it and you have more things to do.

By doing this every single day, you will stretch yourself, and you will force your body into action. Burning unused calories and doing this, especially before you eat food, will cause your body to burn fat stores. If you exercise before eating for the day, your metabolism has not kicked on. So, it now thinks that you're still in a state of sleep. So, you will start to burn the fat just as if you were sleeping. This is a tidbit, something I learned along the way, whether it's true or not, or whether you believe it or not, that's up to you. I'm telling you what I do. I'm telling you what has worked. If you try it, it'll work for you. If not, do what you want to do, but I'm telling you this: to build a powerful foundation, you have to exercise, and you've got to put your body through the wringer. You've got to sweat. That's the next thing in your foundation.

Now, immediately after exercising, I'm ready to refuel and get myself into a state of power. After a powerful exercise, your body is ready for hydration and nutrients. It is ready to consume anything and the first thing it consumes, it will use. So, there's nothing more powerful to put into your body when you come from a powerful exercise than green juice. Putting a powerful green juice into your body right after an exercise sends all of those nutrients and everything valuable to the places that need it. This window is absolutely critical for me to only digest good things. This ain't the time for a Mc-Nothing! Would you put low-octane gas from some side street station into a Ferrari race car? Hell fucking no. If you had a Lamborghini, would you get your oil changed at a raggedy junkyard fix-it shop? Absolutely not. You would put premium, high-octane fuel from a well-established brand and take that car to the dealer for service. That's what you need to do with the most important machine you will ever own. Fresh organic fruits and vegetables, or if you want simple like me, choose a premium powdered green drink mix. This is easy to do, and things that are easy tend to get done. I have a few recipes and suggestions that I will update on getmyS.H.I.T.together.com. Here, I can show you exactly what it is that I use and the supplements that I take. Proper fuel is critical. Putting that fuel into your body at that time will now give you everything you need to feel empowered and build that part of your foundation so that you can have what you need to move forward.

Leaving that space, I'm powered up. I'm ready to think. What do I gotta get done? What moves me forward? Now, I need to take in some powerful ideas to share with others. I need to take in something that's going to get me into a mindset of business. I'm reading a book. I'm reading 10 pages, 20 pages, or listening to an audiobook throughout the morning when I'm running, when I'm working, or right after I'm drinking my smoothie. So, by consuming some powerful information about the business, I am now setting myself up for the exploration of ideas. I'm taking in the best ideas of others who are in my field of business or people who are doing things that interest me around business. I'm not reading romance novels or interesting stories about whales, only business. Anything that doesn't pertain to business is not on the list. I am focusing only on things that pertain to me improving my knowledge and skills around business. How do I make more money? How do I save what I've got? How do I grow what I've got? How do I protect what I've got?

That's what I'm doing. I'm pouring this type of information into my mind to ensure that I am worldly, I'm being efficient, and I can move my business forward. Now, just to make sure that I know exactly what I'm talking about and that I understand it, I declare what it is. By writing down or creating a video to share with others on whatever I learned from the study, 'I know that I know' the lesson from what I heard or I read. And I do it in such a way that if someone were to pick it up, they would also know it too. And, for building the book of Lerrod Smalls, I write it down in a separate journal so that I have left a cookie crumb of knowledge for anyone who would pick it up, even if it's my future self that needs reminding me of the genius level shit that made me great.

POW! And just like that, I have built my foundation. I was taught as a child that a good person tithes ten percent of what they have to the church, so I use that same formula for myself. I dedicate the very first ten percent of the day, two and a half hours, to myself. I'm worth it. You are worth it.

Following this routine, you are now ready to act, and the best tool to set your priorities for the day is an action map. Checkout my daily action map template on getmySHITtogether.com, which will help you dominate your targets for the day and connect with the person who will help get it done. Accountability is critical. If you can get others to know exactly what it is that you're up to, and they can hold you accountable or support you and help you to get to it, that helps get S.H.I.T. done.

A mentor once told me that anything that gets measured gets managed, and things that get managed get done. So, if you can measure whatever it is that you need to do in an action map and manage it by having others around you and hold you accountable and support, that S.H.I.T. will get done. By doing exactly what I just shared with you and doing it in the order that I shared it with you, you will have a routine that is predictable and consistent. It will ultimately become a habit without even thinking about it. Just like you get up and unconsciously brush your teeth in the morning, you must run through a powerful routine every day. You will now be able to consistently and predictably create a productive day. With this process, you can be assured to have a powerful start to whatever it is you want to do with your day. If right now is the time for you to get your S.H.I.T. together, this is the routine that will cause you to do it.

I'm sharing this with you because it works. I know that it works because it has worked for me. And it has worked for thousands of other people. I have crystallized hundreds of hours of books, thousands of hours of application, and tons of stories of people who have used this, and it has worked for them. I cannot tell you how gravity works, why the sun rises in the east, or why women always want what you're eating when they could have ordered the same thing, but I can tell you this process works. Every time. Here is my routine to use as an example or starting point; simply adjust for your lifestyle.

Morning Routine 2024

- **5:15 AM:** WAKE UP / Bathroom / Water / Coffee
- **5:30 AM:** Meditation/ Gratitude Messages
- **6:00 AM:** Cardio - Fit Routine
- **7:00 AM:** Sauna, Reading,
- **7:30 AM:** Formation / Journaling
- **8:00 AM:** Fuel - Green Juice

- **8:15 AM:** Shower, Shave, Dress
- **9:00 AM:** Complete Score Card
- **9:15 AM:** Work

Be Grateful

Before you get something new, this world has a way of making sure you are first grateful for what you have now. The universe will give a stiff chin-check to an ungrateful mother fucker really quick. You might not be where you want to be now, but I guarantee you that it could be a lot worse. I don't care if you are reading this from a jail cell in the world's toughest prison; I promise it can still get worse. You may be thinking that you hate your situation; meanwhile, someone somewhere would gladly switch places with you. A friend told me if everyone in the world could put their life problems into a pile to switch with others, most people would be happy just to pick theirs back up. So, you are not as messed up as you think. It's all about perspective. Having an attitude of gratitude creates the right energy for the work you have to do yourself. When I changed my energy to being grateful for the good things I had going, the rest of my life started to shift. That means no sad songs and pity parties are acceptable. If you woke up today, then you are better off than the 332,648 poor souls who didn't (as per Alexa). And even when you feel beat to hell as you go through this process, remember, if you can look up, then you can get up!

"Ya'll gotta stop with all that "I can't catch a break" bullshit.

All the time you spend complaining, you could be out hustling...

Out chasing your dream."

- Joe Rogan.

You must also be ready to forgive yourself and love yourself before you can become someone new. If not, you will create another version of the unhappy person you are right now. You can't be Grateful and Hateful at the same time. So just accept whatever has happened up to this point as required experiences for what you have coming.

My goal in this process is to help you make your next move, your best move; your next move should be embracing gratitude!

For clarity, being grateful for your S.H.I.T. is not about being complacent or settling for less. It's about recognizing the good in your life and using it as fuel to push forward toward your goals. When you focus on what you're thankful for, you attract more positivity and abundance into your life.

Darren Hardy, the author of "The Compound Effect," says that "gratitude is the gateway to happiness and success." It's not just about feeling grateful, but it rewires your brain to focus on opportunities and possibilities instead of problems and obstacles. When you're grateful, you're more likely to see the silver lining in tough situations and come up with creative solutions.

So, instead of complaining about what you don't have, start appreciating what you do have. It could be something as simple as a roof over your head, food on the table, or the support of loved ones. When you start counting your blessings, you'll realize that you're richer than you think.

Now, I'm not saying that gratitude is a magic solution to all your problems. It's not going to instantly make your dreams come true or erase all of your struggles. But what it will do is provide the right mindset to choose worthy aspirations. When people have a grateful spirit, they're motivated, confident, and resilient. You will be less likely to give up when things get tough because you are so appreciative of what you have now.

So, my challenge to you is to start a gratitude practice today. It could be as simple as writing down three things you're grateful for each morning or evening. Or you could make it a daily habit to express your appreciation to someone who's helped you or made a positive impact on your life. Whatever it is, commit to it and stick with it.

Remember, gratitude is not just a once-in-a-while feeling but a way of life. It's about embracing the present moment and finding joy in the journey. So, be grateful for your S.H.I.T. because it's what's shaping you into the person you're meant to be. And, with a grateful heart, you'll be unstoppable in achieving your dreams and living your best life.

Tribe UP

Humans are community creatures. People thrive better when they are part of a pack like wolves or pride like lions. Everyone is born with innate talents we can offer to the group. As a unified force, we get more powerful results together than we can achieve alone. Men require tribesmen, but choosing the right men is a process of elimination that you can't afford to get wrong. You are your tribe, and your tribe is you.

The people you talk to every day have the biggest influence on your decisions, so it stands to reason that you should surround yourself with people who you want to be more like. Many of us tend to spend our time around people who are something like us ... people who look like us, talk like us and make about the same money as us. If we continue to surround ourselves with people who are just like us, we end up staying just like us. The moment that you decide that you want to **Be** more, **Have** more, and **Do** more, you have to surround yourself with some new people. You have to die who you are and give birth to who you will become. Now, the problem with hanging around the same old people is they constantly want to remind you of who you were and the same old things ya'll used to do.

There's a well-known concept to describe the mentality of certain people in a group called 'crabs in a barrel.' Why is it that you never need to keep a cover on the top of a barrel full of crabs? Because once one crab tries to climb out of the barrel, another crab would see him and automatically grab him and try to pull him back down into the barrel. Even if he tried and almost got out, the crabs would do everything but kill him and rip him apart so that he stayed in the barrel with the rest of the crabs.

Now, that's a natural reaction for crabs and also a very unspoken reaction for people. People do this. People do this unconsciously. Without even realizing that they're doing it, they're doing it. They don't want you to go past where they are because they feel like you will leave them. They'll feel like they will be alone. They'll feel like they lost their friend because, in truth, they have. They have lost that person who you were, and now you're someone new, and they will accuse you of being brand new.

I was accused of being brand new every time I grew in my life and in my business. Every time that I changed and elevated myself, people accused me of being fake and brand-new, and I loved it. I know that I'm evolving and succeeding when people tell me that I've changed because I have not come this far to be the same. And I will not stop here either because I haven't come this far just to come this far. The people around you will either be a steppingstone for you to rise up or a weight on your neck holding you down.

Without proper training, men will divide themselves based on the things that they like. If you connect yourself with people around things that you like, you will have a very frivolous and casual set of relationships because things you like are subject to change. What you liked as a five-year-old is not the same as what you like as a ten-year-old, as a twenty-year-old, or as a thirty-year-old. See, the things that you like will continually change with your feelings, emotions, and interests.

However, your core values are the things that have been embedded deep into the programming you received as a child that makes you who you are ... Is stealing okay for me? Is lying okay for me? Is going to church okay for me? See, these core values are the things that tightly bond people together because they dictate your beliefs around major decisions and regular habits. Men can thrive in partnerships and friendships with people of different opinions as long as they have aligning core values.

The powerful thing about selecting people based on their values is many of them will be outside of your neighborhood, racial group, or religion. These people are called your community, who live in the same environment as you, are familiar with the things you know, do the same things you do, and talk the same talk. But they can't offer you anything new. Now, someone outside of your community can expose you to new ideas and give you opportunities that you didn't have access to. However, they may have different desires and likes and opinions from you, whether they're political, socioeconomic, or just about sports teams. You don't want to separate yourself from people just because they have a different opinion from you because then you'll have a very small group of people who will surround themselves with you, who will be just the way you are right now. Inside that community, you will have an even a smaller group of people who you choose to connect with most frequently, and that's your circle.

The thing I know about a circle is that if you are the brightest one in your circle, you need a new circle. These people may be very committed to keeping life the way they know it exactly the same when you are ready to make a change. It is a fact that you cannot change a person's mind that doesn't want to.

"A man forced against his will is of the same opinion still."

-Les Brown

If you can't change **the people** around you, then you must change **the people who** are around you. As soon as I understood this, I decided to surround myself with people who were a few steps ahead of me, because it gave me somewhere to look. When you surround yourself with people who are a step behind, you find yourself looking back. Not to disrespect those comrades - you've come up with and the people who you love and connect with. Many of them will be family and friends who will always be down for you. But when it comes to moving forward in your life, they must be willing to run with you.

The great Jim Rhon used to say, "I can run with 200, but I can't carry two on my back." Don't find yourself carrying people with you. You're going to have to go to war with yourself, your environment, and some of the people from your old circle. If you're not willing to break some eggs, you'll never have an omelet, and it's definitely time for breakfast. The next big question is who you choose for this power circle that you must create.

Choose People Wisely

We often make connections with people based on superficial bullshit. We latch onto common interests as if they are the foundation of a real connection, but those things are not enough. Common interests can only sustain a relationship for so long, and soon, you will be left with nothing but a bunch of casual and meaningless acquaintances. What you like today may not be what you like tomorrow, next year, or in the next damn decade! Your values, on the other hand, are what matters. Your core beliefs are the principles that define your character. These are what guide your decisions and have shaped you into the person you are today. When people share similar values, they build lasting connections based on things that matter most with others.

Your circle is your community, and you will only excel to the level of your community. When you build a relationship with people from different backgrounds and opinions, but share the same value system as a foundation, you have a tribe. You must surround yourself with people who have the same critical belief system as you, which are values, and genuinely want you to succeed as much as themselves.

The thing is, most of the time, those people won't be in your proximity circle. The guys you grew up with or coworkers on the job. Your tribe is made up of handpicked Kings, not discriminated based on race, religion, or geographical location. True tribesmen will find a way to connect and support each other because they desire trust, respect, and commitment as much as you. Having the same DNA makes you relatives, and having the same values makes you family.

The fundamental truth is that everybody is different, so we think/believe differently. But how do you decide who stays in your life and who is not for you?! Opinions are subject to change because they are based on feelings and how we perceive things at that time. Our Values are the CORE Beliefs of what's important to us and what we prioritize in our lives. I see many people in today's heated political climate destroying relationships with people who share powerful common values just because they have different political opinions... Is that You? Are you holding on to relationships with people that are bad for you and not in alignment with your values just because you like the same fucking football team?

People who can expose you to new ideas, opportunities, and perspectives are like diamond mines. Now, I'm not saying you should cut off anyone who disagrees with you or has a different opinion. Hell no! But you need to think about who is in your circle right now, who's willing to go to battle with you and push you to become a better version of yourself. If you're the brightest one in your circle, then you need to find a new circle because there's no more room for growth.

Opinions are like assholes; everyone's got one, and they're generally full of shit. The only thing that matters is your values, your core beliefs, and your principles. Relationships are necessary, but when it's time for you to get your S.H.I.T. together, only the right relationships matter. You must make the choices because no one can choose these important influences for you. Some people will be willing to grow with you and support you, and you will be able to move forward with them. But the naysayers, the ones who don't share your core values, who drag you down and hold you back, you gotta let those motherfuckers go.

Stop holding onto relationships that are bad for you just because you have a few similar opinions or common interests. It's time to level up, to surround yourself with people who are going to push you to be better, who share your values, and who will be there with you in the trenches. THINK THAT THROUGH and choose your tribe wisely!

The Bottom Line

Getting your S.H.I.T. together is a commitment. You are your habits and your routines. If you want to change anything, you've got to change what you do daily. This is not a one-time thing. You've got to work on yourself consistently and continuously.

You can't be hateful when you're grateful. Stop whining about what you don't have and be thankful for what you do have. Trust me, someone somewhere would love to be in your shoes. If you woke up today, that's a blessing right there. So be grateful and stop singing sad songs. Keep your energy right for the work you've got to do on yourself.

You must forgive yourself and love yourself before you can become someone new. You can't be grateful and hateful at the same time. Accept what has happened up to this point and use it to shape your future.

Now, let's talk about connections. We often build relationships based on superficial stuff. We think having the same hobbies or rooting for the same sports team means something. But it doesn't. It's not about what you like it's about what you value. Your core values are what matters, and those are what should guide your relationships.

You've got to level up your circle. Your tribe should be handpicked kings who share your core values and genuinely want you to succeed as much as themselves. It doesn't matter if they come from different backgrounds or have different opinions. If they share your values, they're your tribe.

Too many people are destroying relationships over different opinions. Opinions change. Values don't. Are you holding onto relationships that are bad for you just because you have a few similar opinions or interests? It's time to level up.

You've got to surround yourself with people who are going to push you to be better, who share your values, and who will be there with you when times get tough. Your tribe is crucial to getting your S.H.I.T. together, so choose wisely.

Alright, we're done here. Now, it's time to take what you've learned and put it into action.

The Cost of Big S.H.I.T.

—The More I Want,

The More I Must become to obtain It

—The More I Receive,

The More I must be worthy to keep it

—The More I Learn,

The More I must be willing to share it

- Lerrod Smalls

Keeping your S.H.I.T. Together

When I said you can do this, King, I meant it. And if you have listened to this audio or read the book, and it has meant something to you, maybe there's someone else just like you, who doesn't know they can get their S.H.I.T. together. So, my only request is you pass this on. Tell them to get their own copy because anytime that someone puts money on the wood, everything is all good. And it'll force them to read it.

Now, get after it. Close this book. Go get your S.H.I.T. together. and I'll see you on the next step, where we RISE!

The Goal is to Learn, Earn, and Return!

- Dr. George C. Fraser

Don't forget, I will always be with you; Salute King.

www.GetMyShitTogether.com

ANTHEMS

With the help of my brother Sherod "Sha Stimuii" Khaalis we created some music that embodies the stories and concepts shared in this book. I included the lyrics to a few of our favorites.

We hope you enjoy the ride.

CALL of DUTY

War is conflict. War can be constant.

War is what happens when your life is full of hardships.

You declare war when you have to take action

Against the opposing faction that ain't utilizing God's gifts.

And that faction is you inside of this war scene.

Now, just imagine if black men were a sports team,

Lower-incomes, high imprisonments, poor mental health,

No generational wealth, and we divorce queens. - shoot each other.

Brothers we're losing, killing our offspring

before the game starts, We're down 114.

Drug addiction morphine. Cops want us gone clean.

What are you doing each day to achieve your dream?

In my life, I was the enemy, fighting temptation.

So many distractions, so much devastation.

Marriage wasn't tight because every night was celebration.

Shorty blowing up my phone and the cheating was detonation.

Salt resembles sugar when you see it from afar, and I was still salty and
cash-spending.

Imagine trying to uphold your image.

So you push a fancy car, but you search for loose change to put gas in it.

I had to stop!

Anthems

Let me be clear. I don't preach like Eric Thomas
And no I'm not an expert. I'm not Tony Robbins.
I ain't clean like Darren Hardy. I curse like the worst.
I have angry outbursts, but now at least I'm fucking honest!
Had to get my shit together.

Get my shit together,
Get my shit together. What's a storm to a God that can fix the weather?
Get my shit together. Get my shit together.
I changed the world through my seeds. I can live forever.

Get your shit together. Get your shit together.
What's a storm to a God that can fix the weather?
Get your shit together. Get your shit together.
Change the world through your seeds. You can live, live forever.

My mother died of cancer after years of paying ties.
Left the congregation. All my faith in God had died,
Made it out of college. Started bringing in some dollars

Until I lost my job on Wall Street and took a crazy dive.
Money bounced back. I thought my life was dope,
Making six figures, always spitting, righteous quotes,
Looking at the world through a telescope to try to cope.
I should have been looking at myself, looking through a microscope,

Get My S.H.I.T. Together

And if I took a deeper look, I would see my wife considering leaving,

But I wasn't shook. I ran my kingdom like a rook.

Drinking whiskey like I'm hooked and picking movies over books. I've

been a criminal and crook.

And then I had a name brand obsession. My business went sour.

I was blaming the recession, giving up my power

By complaining about my blessings. And then we got a phone call. My

daughter's school gave me a lesson.

They let me know off top, they needed dough

or they was about to let her go.

And for me, that hit a sore spot, Because all that fake balling had me

falling into debt.

So I took the chain hanging from my neck and looked for pawn shops.

My whole life was a fictional facade.

If you saw me shining all that shine was a mirage.

I was gaining weight, putting bullshit on my plate.

People called me Smalls and I felt small, but I was large.

Had to get my shit together.

Get my shit together.

What's a storm to a God that can fix the weather.

Get my shit together. Get my shit together.

I changed the world through my seeds. I can live forever.

Anthems

Get your shit together. Get your shit together.
What's a storm to a God that can fix the weather?
Get your shit together. Get your shit together.
Change the world through your seeds. You can live forever.

Get my shit together. It's just like reading a map.
It sounds real simple until you ignore the facts
That you can't get directions to a final destination
If you don't acknowledge your location and where you're at.

You might walk around, like you got it all together, but that could be a
fantasy
Or you just making up a story so you get the fame and glory.
What's your real relationship with your family?
Are you emotionally invested in the ones that you are in bed with

Or are you just sexing them casually?
Because that will be like you deep in the war and the women that you
enter are the trophies.
So they all become casualties.
I don't want to judge you, but it's up to you to do the work gradually

Until you're mad at you like I was mad at me.
Are you truly honest with yourself about the food that you're digesting?
Do you avoid working out more actively?
I had to fertilize my own lawn before I ask about yours.

Get My S.H.I.T. Together

My household was a catastrophe.

I ain't know my kids' favorite colors. I ain't know they shoe sizes

A provider is what I thought a dad should be.

But actually, a father does more than supporting financially

And the husband shows emotion. I was filled up with apathy.

I peeped.my connection with the source was staticky.

The cause of all my issues always pointed right back to me.

Every single battle in this war I was winless until

I focused on my faith to redesign my business.

Loved up, all my family, regimented, my fitness

Made my to-Do list longer than my wishlist.

You are now a witness of how I faced the mirror.

Got to drive like I was Lyfted, recognized, I'm gifted.

Whatever the shit is - that's holding you back,

Don't ignore it like it's distant, this instant.

Get it together!

TRIBE UP

When you declare war, that's putting everyone on notice.

But before you battle, you got to handle some components.

Weapons, strategy, the soldiers in your army,

You're honestly more report than whoever's your opponent.

I challenge you today to please look at your circle.

Are your acquaintances there to help you or hurt you?

Are you letting in people that are only feeding your ego?

How do friend interactions truly serve you?

Who's in your army? Do the people that surround you

Lift you up and at the same time ground you?

Are they holding you accountable and also holding you down

too. if you were down two, with two seconds left on the clock,

Would you pass them to rock, to take the shot?

Please look at your circle.

Are those people coming to your performance or they coming to your rehearsals?

Be careful. Who's running the race with you? The same person handing you the baton, might be the one creating the hurdles.

Tribe up king, who's in your tribe?

Now's the time. Ask yourself who's inside of this life that you've created.

Who's holding those spots that are so sacred?

Are the people close to you causing you to shed blood just because y'all are blood-related?

And are they congratulating or hating?

Who's next to you when you are waking?

Can you trust those souls that see you when you are exposed?

Would you put your life in the hands of whoever's seeing you naked?

Who's in your tribe? KING, you might hear me, but I hope you listen.

The world is yours, but there's a part in that Quote that's missing.

Your world is literally yours. Your universe, your galaxy,

Your solar system, and that star that's shining and providing that energy for everything that moves.

That's you. And those planets that's revolving in your orbit getting light are they bringing you good fortune. That's who?

Who's in your tribe? King.

Huh?

Figure that out.

Yeah.

Tribe up.

So your loved ones are who you're feeding with urgency,

And they call on you when there might be an emergency.

If you got a health issue or needed some currency right there, that's your Venus and your Mercury

Anthems

And in your earth, your foundation, which you might consider being the
friend zone,

They're with you in every practice, scrimmage and huddle,
And they should be there when you get to the end zone.
So when you touch down on that journey, they should celebrate with you.
Man. You might need to adjust your headphones.

This is where it gets rude. Some of y'all will let fools talk you into stalling,
Man....
Stalling is for the restroom. I told you, that you a star.
So watch that person lurking in your space like he's on Mars when he
should be on Neptune.
Look at just Circle King. I applaud you.

Don't just hang with that woman that adores you, caters to you, makes
you feel good.
What feels good isn't always good for you.
So it's cool to be around people that move just like you, that are your
type,
But place the people close to you that you want to be more like elders,
mentors,

Someone in your field that has done what you're trying to do with your
life.
Your tribe is your community. They share your environment.
The brothers you can trust, the ones that you're confided in.

Pay close attention to the soldiers that are standing by your left and right shoulders in the war.

That's who you riding with. The ones that will grow with you, the boys that will better you, challenge you, support you,
Maybe a step ahead of you. Somebody that's achieving with moves that's so incredible.
Your whole tribe being successful … is inevitable.
Tribe above king.

1440

Key to life. The present is a gift.
There's nothing you can find that's more important in this world.
Then time, 24 hours to go get it each day.
That's fourteen hundred and forty minutes.

Every minute is so costly.
That's that 1440. We call it 1440.
So what you doing with your 1440 King?

We all came in this world without possessions.
No flashy jewels or crazy whips, little humans just crying to get attention
Before we focus on copping the latest kicks.
It doesn't matter your heritage or complexion.
Your fam could be poor. They may be rich, but you've been favored since your conception.
The creator provided the greatest gift.

Time is the treasure. Seconds come first. Minutes are your money.
You measuring your worth by your salary amount or the bread in your account
With there's value in the moments ever since your birth, every single day.
You got 1440. Don't sit around drinking fourteen 40s,
different baby mamas got 14 shortys
Stop acting like you 14, when you pushing 40.

The present is a gift.
There's nothing you can find that's more important in this world and time,
24 hours to go get it, - each day
That's fourteen hundred and forty minutes. Every minute is so costly.
That's that 1440. We call it 1440.
So what you doing with your 1440?

Don't waste time on Netflix, YouTube, PlayStation, Xbox, Instagram, Facebook, Snapchat, TikTok.
Entertain yourself if that's important. But don't spend hours swiping and scrolling, Look at your wristwatch.

Put the phone down, drop the remote.
Lose the controller that's controlling you the most.
Experience your life instead of living through your posts.
Every second counts.- Yo, my mother had a quote.

Focus on the pennies and the dollars will be fine.
I'm paraphrasing that. But if you related to time, she meant make the best out of every little minute, your hours start to shift and your days will be divine.
When I wake up, before I start the grind, I map out my 1440 inside my mind,
How I'm about to spend it, who I need to visit.
But the first two and a half hours are all mine.

Anthems

I believe in charity. I believe in investing.

I believe giving to others is a blessing.

Even though your fam and friends might be requesting,

you got to make time for you.

You can put money on an inmate's books and commissary. Just think about that for some seconds.

Would someone locked up want a gift that's monetary or would they rather some time off of their sentence?

1440- 1440 dudes sit around drinking fourteen 40s

different baby mamas like 14 shortys

Stop acting like you're 14 when you're pushing 40.

Get your shit together.

THE FORMULA

You want to know how to win the war
And how to be better than you were the day before.
The formula, the strategy, the daily techniques
That you need to put in place when you walk outside your doors.

Every human being gets the same. 24.
Nobody's time is more important than yours.
You start by waking early. You produce strong results
when you use the whole day, it feels like you're working with more.

Here's the routine. This will shape your attitude
To set off each morning, so the day is not attacking you.
You attack the day. You don't have to kneel to pray,
But be thankful out loud for your blessings, Express gratitude

And then you let go of the waste. - in your system.
Let it out and then go and replace that waste with the water
That you need as your base hydration, lubrication for your whole mental
space.

Here's the blueprint. You want to know how to win the war,
How to be better than you were the day before.
Everybody breathing gets the same. 24.
I'm going to show you how to get so much more out of yours.

Anthems

Next step. This might encounter hesitation.
See, men get the wrong idea of guided meditation,
But all you're really doing is quieting your mind
And clearing the runway for your flight and your elevation.

It's like your desk gets cluttered or your closet is a mess.
Your thoughts stretch more when they're surrounded by less
Worries about bills or financial stress.
You can silence all that and give social media a rest.

You should be selective with whatever you choose to enter your mental,
Treat your energy just like your residential. That's where you live.
Next thing is to grab a pen or a pencil.
If your phone is the memo that you vent to, then use that.

Keep a journal with whatever's on your heart,
A list of things you're grateful for. Just find somewhere to start
Or stuff you need to do, maybe broken down in parts.
Send notes of gratitude to some people. Create some art.

See, this is priceless. You want to know how to win the war,
How to be better than you were the day before.
Everybody breathing gets the same. 24.
I'm going to show you how to get so much more out of yours.

After showing love to everyone you.

When your Karma is cool, the one that's in the mirror,

Now you got to give him the fuel and activate your senses.

If it's exercise or stretching, put your body through some pressure.

It's the most important tool, and if you like me

And you want that mean boost right after the workout,

I'm guzzling some green juice. Get my shit together dot com if you want the ingredients.

High octane gas is what you fill your Lamborghini with.

Never treat your temple like a rental for no reason.

The last part of my routine and why I'm succeeding,

Gratitude meditation journal, exercise.

You add nourishment and then it's an audio book or reading,

Consuming what I need to add inside of my recipe

And write some notes down so they stick inside of my memory.

Find your process, find your method, do something.

Just be consistent and the war for the day is yours!

ABOUT THE AUTHOR

Lerrod Smalls is a man on a Mission. Forged by the grittiest parts of Brooklyn, NY, and conditioned by tough parents to be both street and book smart. Programmed full of life experiences to overcome the struggle and fight to make a way, his journey from the corners to college to a corporate job was the pinnacle of his aspirations until he found his place as a serial entrepreneur. Lerrod became the first millionaire in his family before 30, earning high recognition & results, only to be matched by his tragic fall into bankruptcy and depression.

From Triumph to Tragedy, with a marriage on the edge of divorce, being a disconnected Father, unhealthy & overweight, and a failed businessman, Lerrod realized he was on a direct path to fulfilling the same destiny as many Black

Men in his community. Suffering. After years of sacrifice and commitment to change through mentorship, he discovered a new code.

A warrior's code.

Armed with a new way of Being, Believing, and Living, he was reincarnated as a new man with radically different results. Lerrod reclaimed financial success through real estate and coaching, forged a new loving relationship with his family that he is proud of, and became a world-champion Jiu Jitsu fighter at age 46, proving it is never too late to create a life worth living.

Compelled to share the formula for this transformation, Lerrod founded the Black Warrior King Tribe and launched Rise of the Black Warrior as a resource to eliminate self-sabotage regardless of the unique challenges facing his community. Lerrod has since expanded his coaching and mentorship to support many diverse groups of people searching for a lighthouse of truth.

Through the Podcast, Videos, and Training Programs, he intends to plot a new course for men with a proven code for living that they must Shake Up, Wake Up, and Rise Up to be Kings.